An Introduction to SFC Models Using Python

Brian Romanchuk

Published by BondEconomics, Canada

www.BondEconomics.com

Published by BondEconomics, 2017, Montréal, Québec.

Library and Archives Canada
An Introduction to SFC Models Using Python
Brian Romanchuk 1968-
ISBN 978-1-7751676-1-7 Epub Edition
ISBN 978-1-7751676-0-0 Kindle Edition
ISBN 978-0-9947480-9-6 Paperback Edition

Contents

Acknowledgements

I would like to thank the readers of my articles at BondEconomics.com for their feedback. Portions of this text previously appeared as articles on that site, and I have been able to incorporate suggestions and corrections.I would also like to thank Judy Yelon for her editing of this text.

Finally, any errors and omissions are my own.

Chapter 1 Introduction

1.1 Introduction

Stock-Flow Consistent modelling (SFC modelling) is a popular class of economic models used by post-Keynesian economists. The models emphasise the rigorous modelling of national accounting data. However, the models go beyond just tracking national accounts, and include behavioural equations. The hope is that by modifying these behavioural equations, the stock-flow consistent models can capture the key behaviour of the mathematical models that have been developed by the various post-Keynesian schools of thought.

The difficulty with stock-flow consistent modelling is that the act of capturing the interactions of all sectors implies a combinatorial explosion of the number of equations within the model. Even extremely simple models of the economy can result in dozens of equations if we incorporate international trade, since we need to model the economy of more than one country. The mass of equations acts as a distraction from the economic logic.

The Python *sfc_models* framework was developed as a means to reduce the mathematical burden of dealing with SFC models. The user specifies the high-level description of the economy, and the framework generates the underlying equations (and attempts to solve them). It is straightforward to make a change to the structure of the model and then jump to see the resulting effect on economic variables. Even if we cannot fit the model to real-world data to use as a forecasting tool, we can use the models to generate ideas regarding predictable relationships between economic variables.

This book describes the *sfc_models* package, and acts an introduction to Python and SFC modelling. Since there is already a large amount of Python tutorial material available, this book attempts to explain how Python differs from other programming languages and offers a starting point for more advanced topics. It is hoped that the example code should provide a good starting point for users who are comfortable with other programming languages.

The models discussed in the book are largely based on a single textbook – *Monetary Economics* by Wynne Godley and Marc Lavoie. That textbook is a standard introduction to SFC modelling, and models within it have already been implemented in other computer languages. This was advantageous, as it was possible to calibrate the *sfc_models* output to match those other implementations. Therefore, the model outputs discussed in this book are hardly novel, rather the difference is how the models are determined and solved. Since the models are well known, the description of how they work is held to the minimum. The descriptions are aimed at those who are unfamiliar with SFC models, as how the models operate may be surprising to those new to the field.

1.2 The Python SFC Model Workflow

The way in which the *sfc_models* package is typically used is distinctive. The objective is to focus the user's attention upon the linkages between sectors of the economy and not on the drudgery of national accounting. It is a preliminary computer-aided design (CAD) package for economics.

The steps involved in using the package are as follows. This section offers an overview of these steps; the rest of the book fills out the detail.

1. The Python code imports the *sfc_models* package.

2. The user then creates *objects* that represent the economic sectors. (There is an explanation of what is meant by *objects* below.) Behavioural parameters are specified, and the linkages between the sectors.

3. Once the objects are created, the model-building operation of the *sfc_models* framework is invoked.

4. The framework generates the equations that specify the model based on the sector object properties. These equations are specified within a text block that is output to log files that can be examined by the user.

5. The framework then invokes an equation solver that takes as an input the equations in text form. It then generates time series outputs, assuming that it can find a solution to the system of equations. (If the user's specifications of the economic sectors

are missing linkages or are internally inconsistent, there may not be a solution. Alternatively, the user may have specified behavioural relationships that are beyond the capacity of the solver.)

6. The framework then saves the time series as a text-delimited file ("csv file"), as well as Python objects that can be further analysed using other Python code. For example, the time series plots in this report were created using the *matplotlib* Python package.

At the time of writing, this workflow relies upon the user running Python code. This need not be complex; the reader is free to invoke example code that is provided to generate the output that matches what is displayed in this report. Once the *sfc_models* code is sufficiently advanced, it should be possible for the user to specify the configuration of economic sectors within the model by using a graphical user interface (GUI). In other words, it would be possible to build a model with "drag and drop" operations within a window. This would allow students to examine a variety of economic models and see how they behave as conditions change. Such an approach would allow a more hands on approach to learning, and not rely upon following others' interpretations of how the economy works.

Returning to the workflow above, steps 1-3 are implemented by the user, and the framework generally finishes off the operations. That said, the user has control over the remaining steps if desired.

•   The user can take the generated equations, and solve them using other techniques. Since the equations created are visible, the models generated by the framework are not opaque black boxes.

•   The user can generate model equations by hand, and then input the equations into the *sfc_models* solver.

•   The user is free to import the time series data into other software for further processing. For example, loading the data into a spreadsheet is probably the easiest way to look at the behaviour of all the time series within the model solution.

The description above refers to the creation of *objects*. This is not a case of being vague; rather it is using software engineering jargon. In this case, the objects are components of *object-oriented programming*, which may not be familiar to readers who have not studied software engineering, but were instead taught how to program by non-specialists who typically take a *procedural programming* approach.

Under the object-oriented approach, code is created in a modular form, with objects that comprise both the functions that determine behaviour, as well as the data structures associated with those functions. In order to reduce the problems caused by inter-connected code, the objects are designed to be distinct, or inherit properties from parent objects in a hier-archical fashion.

In this case, this means that the code that defines how a sector behaves is independent of the rest of the model. For example, we can modify the behavioural functions defining household behaviour without worrying about the implementation of the business sector. This allows us to make changes without having to worry about unexpected code interactions. If a sector's behaviour depends upon information from another sector, the user just needs to look at the external interface of that sector, without needing to delve into the implementation details of that other sector.

Section 2.4 discusses the differences between object-oriented program-ming and procedural programming.

The advantage of using the *sfc_models* framework is the ease of experi-mentation. The traditional way to develop SFC models is determine the equations to be solved by hand, and then use software to generate the solution. The difficulty with this manual approach is that it is not obvious how to modify equations if you want to make changes to the economic model. Furthermore, the solution is prone to errors, as you need to tran-scribe dozens of equations comprised of variables with similar names to a software package. Conversely, building an economic model using *sfc_models* only requires a handful of lines of user code, and the structure of the code gives a good idea of the structure of the model, even to a non-specialist. Furthermore, the user can see the generated equations, but never needs to work with them manually.

1.3 About this Book

The writing of this book was a calculated gamble. Version 1.0 of *sfc_models* contains what is viewed as a minimal set of economic behaviour in order for the package to be interesting. Since it does not yet even implement all the existing models in Godley and Lavoie's *Monetary Economics*, it is obviously not an extension of the frontiers of stock-flow consistent modelling.

For the *sfc_models* framework to succeed, it will need researchers to extend the functionality beyond what is available in Version 1.0. For someone familiar with Python, such extensions should be easy to do. That is, Version 2.0 could potentially offer a dizzying array of implemented economic behaviours. However, to get to that point, we will need more researchers who understand the overall architecture of *sfc_models*. This book was written as that architecture guide.

It is not expected that all readers of this book will want to work on extending the framework. This book also acts an introductory guide that explains how the code examples work. Even if the objective is to run some code examples in order to understand stock-flow consistent models, the framework should be less of a mysterious black box.

Since the theory of the book is largely based on that contained in one textbook, and the discussions revolve around the code within the *sfc_models* package, there was no need seen for a bibliography or citations.

Code examples are of the format:

File: hello_world.py

```
def main():
    print('Hello World!')

main()
```

The Python language is sensitive to white space (indentation by spaces, and tabs), which is unlike many other computer languages. If there are line breaks in this text, readers may need to be careful if attempting to run code examples. For example, line breaks were introduced to fit on the page, and the risk is that the location of the line break will not match Python syntax standards. Larger examples are incorporated as files within the *sfc_models* package, and those examples should be examined to see the proper syntax to use the package.

Chapter 2 Why Python?

2.1 Introduction

This chapter gives an overview of the Python programming language. It is not meant to be a tutorial for the language; there is already a great deal of introductory materials available elsewhere. Instead, the objective is to outline features that are somewhat distinct to Python when compared to other programming languages.

The *sfc_models* package was implemented in Python for two main reasons. From the author's perspective, the object-oriented programming support is cleaner than some potential competitor languages, and it has the most efficient workflow. (I discuss object-oriented programming in Section 2.4.) The efficiency argument flows from the extremely clean Python syntax, as well as the excellent programming tools that are available.

The fact that Python is open source (free to download) is an advantage when compared to packages like Matlab™ and Eviews, ™ which are extensively used in academia. (As discussed in Section 5.2, the *sfc_models* package was calibrated against the output of models implemented in Eviews. ™) The major open source language competitor is the R programming language, which is probably used much more heavily by economists. In fact, there is an R SFC models package under development. It is found at https://github.com/S120/PKSFC. The R package relies on the user generating the equations, which implies that it would eventually be possible to integrate it and *sfc_models*. However, I am much less comfortable with the R object-oriented framework, and the design of *sfc_models* relies heavily on the object-oriented approach.

If the reader lacks experience with programming, my hope is that they will be at least able to follow the examples and discussion within this book. The objective of the *sfc_models* framework is that the code for models should be clean enough that it would be possible to experiment with the parameters in models without having to understand the details of the implementation. This will allow the reader to do basic analytical exercises with SFC models using Python. However, it is clear some technical sections will be difficult for such readers to follow.

2.2 Installing and Using Python and the Package

Python is an open source programming language, and so it can be downloaded at no cost. The user is free to do what they wish with the software, so long as they follow the terms of the licence agreement. (The *sfc_models* package is also distributed in this fashion.)

I will not offer instructions on how to install Python; the procedures depend upon the computer's operating system. There is a great deal of troubleshooting information available on the internet.

The key decision is whether you wish to download the base Python installation or work with an integrated development environment (IDE). I used to do my Python programming with the IDLE GUI (Graphical User Interface) that is installed by default with Python, but I have switched to using the PyCharm™ development environment by JetBrains: (https://www.jetbrains.com/pycharm/). PyCharm is available in two main editions: a free community edition that is sufficient for most programming and a commercial edition that is aimed at professional software developers. In addition, JetBrains has an edition for learning how to program: the user goes through lessons in steps. (There are other programming platforms available for Python; I am not familiar with them.)

Once you have installed Python, there are three ways of using the language.

1. You can start the Python interpreter, and then type commands that are then processed. This interactive mode is useful for testing, but it is not the preferred way to do complex tasks. This interactive mode is similar to how *Matlab* and *R* are used, but not compiled languages (like C++).

2. You can have the Python interpreter start running a script, and then it processes the commands within the script (Python scripts are files with the extension ".py").

3. You can work with a graphical development environment (IDLE, PyCharm) and develop Python scripts. You then launch the scripts using a command within the GUI. This is the usual way of developing in Python.

The advantage of working with Python scripts (*.py files) is that you can repeat the same steps without having to type them in again.

Once Python is installed, there are two ways of installing the *sfc_models* package: either downloading the latest Python package or by using the *git* source control system.

The easiest method is to load the latest production version that has been uploaded to the Python Package Repository (at *pypi.org*). The package is found at: https://pypi.python.org/pypi/sfc_models/. This download can either be done automatically through PyCharm, or else using the *pip* installation script on the command line.

The use of PyCharm is the simplest solution; you just need to add the *sfc_models* package to the Python installation, as described in the PyCharm documentation.

The slightly more complex solution is to use the *pip* installation script. The script is found in the "*scripts*" subdirectory below the Python installation. From the command line, you just need to run:

```
pip install sfc_models
```

However, you may need to do some steps before running "pip install," and those steps may vary across operating systems. Since these installation methods will change over time, the reader is referred to online documentation on the usage of pip.

Code examples are found in the `sfc_models/examples/scripts` directory. You could find this directory, and copy the files to a working directory. Alternatively, you can run an installation script that is available once *sfc_models* is installed. To do this, open a Python console, and run the following.

```
from sfc_models.objects import *
install_examples
```

Invoking *install_examples* should bring up pop-up windows that ask you where you wish to install the example scripts.

Using source control is discussed in Section 2.6.

2.3 Procedural Programming

One of the pieces of programming jargon previously mentioned is *object-oriented programming*. In order to understand the significance of object-oriented programming, we first need to cover an alternative means of structuring programs – *procedural programming*. Procedural programming is typically how students are introduced to programming, and so might be more familiar to some readers.

Procedural programming is based on building a library of functions, and then generating the desired output by calling those functions. (The name for the programming style comes from *procedures*, which are functions that do not have return values. Since procedures are just a special kind of function, Python does not support them as a concept.)

One of the simplest examples for procedural programming in Python would be the following.

```
def square(x):
    out = x*x
    return(out)

y = 10
y_squared = square(y)
print(y_squared)
```

The code creates a function "square" (starting with the line that starts "def square") and then uses it to calculate the square of 10. The function invocation is the line:

```
y_squared = square(y)
```

The output of the function is assigned to the variable "y_squared." Note that we can use the under-bar character ("_") within variable names, which allows us to build up variable names that have multiple words. This facility is used a lot within the *sfc_models* framework; rather than using cryptic mathematical symbols for economic variables, variables are denoted by multiple components separated by under-bars.

The function definition itself is noteworthy for those of you who are familiar with other languages. The start of a function is marked by a def statement of the following format:

```
def {function name}(variable list):
```

The code that implements the function is defined by the indented lines that follow the `def` statement (in this case, the two following lines). We can indent lines with tabs or space characters, so long as the indentation method is consistent. As soon as we hit lines that are not indented, we have exited the function definition. This is different from other languages, where some form of marker denotes the end of a function. (For example, the function code is the block of code between "{" and "}" in other languages like R.) The advantages of the Python idiom are three-fold.

1. We do not waste our time typing unnecessary code block characters.
2. In order for code to function, it has to be indented in a consistent fashion. (In software development, a remarkable amount of time is lost debating code indentation practices.)
3. We do not have to track down bugs caused by missing code block characters.

The only "disadvantage" of the Python dependence upon *white space* is that new programmers are no longer free to use random indentation in their code. (White space are characters that do not appear on the printed page, rather they control the placement of other characters. The space, tab, and end of line characters are the most common white space characters.) When looking at the previous discussion, this is actually a good thing, but it does mean that programmers used to languages that are more lenient may be surprised by the errors they run into. In particular, readers of the ebook version of this book need to be careful if they are typing code as it appears on the reader; line breaks may be introduced which will result in the code not functioning if entered in that fashion. (The issues are caused by allowing the text to "reflow" according to the size of the screen. Reflowing text is well suited to portable reading devices, but it plays havoc with white space.) The printed version of this book should be safer to follow, but formatting may still cause issues. If you are having difficulties getting code to run, there is a large amount of example code that shows the proper syntax. Larger blocks of example code are installed with the *sfc_models* package, and these are the definitive source.

Python supports procedural programming, but this programming style runs into limitations once we have code that is more complex. Object-oriented programming arose as a way to handle those difficulties, as is discussed next.

2.4 Object-Oriented Programming

In object-oriented programming, code is no longer organised around libraries of functions, instead we work with "objects." Objects naturally tie together data structures and the functions that operate on those structures.

As an example of the issues involved, I will use an example that is drawn on my experience with financial libraries. Imagine a function that calculates the price of a bond based on its yield. The minimal version of the function (based on highly simplified bond specifications) would have the following footprint:

```
def bond_price(yield, bond_maturity, bond_coupon,
coupon_frequency):
```

However, this would not be enough for a pricing application; we would need something closer to:

```
def bond_price(yield, bond_maturity, bond_coupon,
coupon_frequency, settle_date, issue_date, yield_
convention, cash_flow_date_convention):
```

That is, we can end up with functions with dozens of parameters.

The situation gets worse when we want to do a calculation that involves not only the bond, but also another instrument (such as a fitted yield curve). Not only do we need parameters to specify the bond structure, we need to pass all of the information describing the other object (the yield curve).

The way to defeat this complexity is to wrap up the data structure and the associated code into a single entity. Within the *sfc_models* framework, the main objects are `Sector` objects, which, as the name suggests, represent the sectors of an economy. By wrapping the sector code into objects, we can simultaneously have easy-to-understand high-level code that works with all of the sectors within a model, yet each sector can have specialised code that implements each sector's specialised rules.

In order to distinguish the functions that are embedded within objects from standard procedural functions, we call the functions within objects *methods*.

The discussion of the object hierarchy in Section 3.4 offers a more concrete example of how this structure is implemented. Additionally, Chapter 7 discusses how researchers can add modelling capability by creating subclasses of existing economic objects. That discussion offers a more concrete explanation of the advantage of the object-oriented approach taken.

Finally, this text often repeats the word *object*. Although this is clumsy, it is a deliberate choice. We need to distinguish entities in code from real world (or theoretical) entities that have the same name. For example, I could discuss the concept of a "sector" as it is used in economics, and then turn to discuss a concrete Sector object that exists in *sfc_models* code. The distinction is reinforced by marking these objects with a special font, and refers to them using their capitalised proper name – as in the previous sentence.

2.5 Programming Tools

The efficiency gains from the Python language and modern development interfaces are not the only selling point; the high quality of the software tools also matters. These tools make the development of the *sfc_models* framework much more robust than would be the case if we relied upon seat-of-the-pants coding.

The first tool is refactoring support, which is available in PyCharm. It is possible to do things such as safely renaming functions – the framework will identify all of the usages of that function within the code base (including example code). This is much less dangerous than relying on a "find and replace" function.

The second tool is the unit testing framework. *Unit tests* are small snippets of code that validate that a function (method) returns an expected output value when called with a particular input. Rather than doing *ad hoc* tests during development, you instead build up a large suite of tests as you build out a function's capabilities. You can then run all of the tests after making a change, to make sure that the change did not break existing functionality. This makes it possible for multiple programmers to work on a project, and have a disciplined way of validating that their code is compatible.

Another tool supports unit testing – *code coverage*. We need to ensure that the entire code base is being tested by unit tests. (If only half of the code base is covered with tests, it is possible that a code change will break code that is not tested.) Code coverage determines which lines are executed in unit tests; the *sfc_models* framework is targeted to remain at 100% coverage. The commercial version of PyCharm has integrated test coverage analysis, but not the free (community) edition. However, it is easy to add coverage tests using the standard Python `coverage` module.

Finally, code complexity measures are useful. No one wants to have to deal with spaghetti code with functions that are thousands of lines long. Code complexity is a measure of how "spaghetti-like" code is; and it can be used to identify which code blocks need to be simplified. (If we have unit tests in place, it is easy to validate that simplifications do not change functionality.) Once again, I have used Python modules to run complexity analysis, as they are not built into the PyCharm community edition.

2.6 Source Control and the Package Repository

Users who are interested in programming are recommended to use the *git* source control system to work with the *sfc_models* package. It is possible to get the latest development version, and it is possible to make changes to the package and have those changes be merged with the project code. If you just download the source code, any changes you make would be overwritten if you downloaded a newer version. However, the installation process is more complex than simply using the latest package.

Using the *git* source control system allows the user to get the latest version of the code from GitHub (a website aimed at sharing code using *git*). The GitHub site offers software for downloading and updating your copy of the code, or it can be done with the *git* command line tools. (You can also download the files as a fixed archive file from GitHub, but updating the software is more difficult.)

The author's copy of the code is found at: https://github.com/brianr747/SFC_models.

There is a certain amount of jargon associated with the *git* source control system. This is a side effect of the system being much more sophisticated than just downloading the source files.

The first piece of jargon is *repository*, which is a copy of code under source control. The version of the code that is found at GitHub is thus a repository; I have other repositories that are versions of the code that is saved locally on my computers.

The preferred way of getting a copy of the code is via *cloning* the repository. This creates a new repository that matches the source repository. If you have an account on GitHub, it is possible to create a clone under your account. This is known as a *fork* of the project. The original repository has led to two repositories, itself, and the new one, and this split can be visualised as a fork in the road. (In some open source environments, the creation of a fork is frowned upon, as it is a sign that the project has split into factions. In the workflow used at GitHub, progress is expected to happen as the result of the creation of forks.)

Once you have a copy of the repository, you need to decide which version of the code to *check out.* The versions of the code are known as *branches.* Within *sfc_models*, the structure is standard: there is the production branch labelled "master," and then the "development" branch. Additionally, there are new branches that represent new work areas, which then are merged into the *development* branch. If the development branch has advanced sufficiently, the new code is pushed into the *master* (production) branch, and that version of the code is then given a new version number. These new *master* versions are then used to update the version of the package on the Python package repository.

The *git* software manages all of the various versions of the code, and tracks changes (so long as they have been *committed* to the local repository). It is possible to jump between the development version and any other version with a single *checkout* command, and then return to your development copy.

In order to get the latest version of the code, you just need to *pull* from the GitHub repository that you cloned. The command line command to do so is:

```
git pull origin development
```

to get the development branch.

The means to collaborate on the project is to use *pull requests.* You would create a public repository on GitHub (under your account) that is cloned from *sfc_models*, and then push your changes to that repository. You can *push* changed code to the repository since you control that repository. In order to get the changes incorporated into the main *sfc_models* repository, you make a pull request – a request to the owner of the main repository (currently myself) to pull the changes into the main code base.

The project owner will review the changes, and decide whether to incorporate them. It will be necessary to understand the programming protocol to be able to insert your own code. However, pull requests can also be used as a communications device, and non-programmers can use them to suggest changes to the project without actually providing new code.

2.7 Python Syntax and the Import Statement

The `import` statement is a key concept in Python. The Python language has only a few commands and data types that are always available for use; most of the complex functionality is embedded in *modules*. A module is a Python file, which usually has the extension ".py" (for source code). In order to use what is found in these modules, we need to import them (with the `import` command). In particular, we need to import the *sfc_models* package code in order to use it. For people who are installing the *sfc_models* package (or the *matplotlib* library, which is used for chart plotting), installation problems will usually show up in the form of an import statement failing.

This book is not meant to be a tutorial on the Python language; there are many tutorials already available. My hope is that readers who are unfamiliar with Python (but know another computer language) will be able to understand how my example code works through experimentation. However, if you do not know how importing code works, you could easily be stuck, and there will be nothing available to help you. For example, if you do not import the *sfc_models* objects – which may be done in a single line of code – every other line of code in the example will fail. The Python errors will not be helpful since the base Python language knows nothing about the *sfc_models* package.

If you open up a Python interpreter, and type "x=y+7" *as the first thing that you do*, you will get a response that resembles the following:

```
>>> x = y + 7
Traceback (most recent call last):
  File "<pyshell#0>", line 1, in <module>
    x = y + 7
NameError: name 'y' is not defined
```

Such a response is not surprising to programmers; you are referring to a variable (y) before it is defined. That will fail in any language. Some languages, such as C, insist that variables be declared, and as being a fixed data type before being used. In Python, you do not declare the variables before you use them, and the type is determined by the initial assignment to the variable. You can change the data type for the variable by another assignment statement.

How function declarations work is perhaps less intuitive. The function definition statement (def) defines a new object that has a name given in the def statement. The following set of commands does an operation that might be impossible to replicate in non-scripting languages.

```
>>> adder = 1.0
>>> type(adder)
<class 'float'>
>>> def adder(x, y):
        return x + y

>>> type(adder)
<class 'function'>
>>> adder(1, 3)
4
```

In the code, we first define "adder" to be a float (with a value of 1.0). We then make a function definition statement ("def adder(x, y):"). (The body of the function is indented; the end of the indentation marks the end of the function.) The type associated with the name "adder" is now "function." Calling adder with arguments x=1, y=3 gives the expected result (4).

As an aside, please note the lack of variable type declaration. This allows the function to attempt to operate on any variables that are passed in. In this case, since strings (class str) support the "+" operator, the following code works.

```
>>> adder('cat', 'fish')
'catfish'
```

Of course, not all possible combinations of inputs are supported by the "+" operator; in such case, there will be some error thrown. For example x = 'a' + 2.0 does not make any sense.

It is possible to use either single quote (') or double quote (") characters to define strings in Python, so long as the closing character matches the opening character. Note that it is necessary to use straight quote characters; if there are any curly quotation characters ("") in example code in this book, that is an error that was introduced in the editing or file transmission process. There is a preference towards single quotes in Python coding standards, but you should use double quotes to define strings with a single quote character in them (or vice-versa). The next snippet shows the flexibility with quote handling.

```
>>> print('a" ' + " b'")
a"  b'
```

.It is also possible to use triple double quotes to define a multi-line string. These are used heavily within internal documentation (document strings that are displayed by the help command).

```
>>> a = """
hello!
multi line
string"""
>>> a
'\nhello!\nmulti line\nstring'
```

(The '\n' character denotes an end-of-line character.)

If we put the Python commands into a file, we get the same results as typing them on the command line (although working in a file is much more efficient). For small scratch programs, we might be able to work entirely with built-in commands and defining functions locally. However, any serious programming task requires us to access code that lies in other modules.

In Python, accessing another module is achieved by the import statement. There are two ways of importing outside code; I will cover them in turn.

The simpler-to-understand syntax is an import statement of the following form: import module_name. For example:

```
>>> import datetime
>>> type(datetime)
<class 'module'>
>>> datetime.date.today()
datetime.date(2017, 3, 31)
```

The first statement imports the datetime module, which is a module that is shipped with all versions of Python. We now have an object named "datetime," which we see has the "module" type. We can now access functions within the datetime object. The example above accesses the "today" function associated with the "date" type (which is defined in the datetime module).

The advantage of this structure is that the "today" function is defined independently of any other function named "today." For example, you could define your own function "today," and it is separate from the function in the datetime module; you have the qualifier "datetime.date" in front to distinguish them.

One thing to note is that we do not supply the file path associated with a module in the import statement; we just use the base part of the file name. This is not just a special property of built-in modules; no import statements use the file path. (If the *sfc_models* package is installed correctly, it is imported in exactly the same way as built-in modules.)

Dealing with user-defined modules outside of installed modules is trickier. For readers who start working the *sfc_models* framework, the usual case is to have all your modules in the same directory. You just use the name of your file, without the ".py" extension.

For example, imagine you have your code in two files, *utils.py* and *work.py*. As the name indicates, the utils.py file contains stand-alone utility functions, and *work.py* needs those functions. In this case, you just insert "import utils" at the top of work.py. (The usual convention is to place imports at the top of a file, even though it would be possible to hold off the import statement until you need to refer to *utils.py*.)

If you have a module with a name that conflicts with another name, you can modify the import statement to assign the module to a new name. This is not normally a problem with built-in modules, since nobody sensible uses the same module name as a built-in for their own modules. However, these module name clashes are more common once we get to user-defined modules.

```
>>> import datetime as foo
>>> foo.date.today()
datetime.date(2017, 3, 31)
```

Having to put the module name in front of functions and objects can be quite cumbersome. If you know that you will not have name clashes, you can import code directly using the second import statement syntax. This version uses "`from {module} import {object}`" to import objects.

This is done quite often in my *sfc_models* example code. For example, you might see:

```
from sfc_models.models import Model
```

This allows us to use the Model object, which is found in the "models" module of *sfc_models*. (The code of *sfc_models* is broken up into separate files – modules – that reside in the package.) We can then write:

```
mod = Model()
```

instead of the more cumbersome:

```
import sfc_models.models
mod = sfc_models.models.Model()
```

One shortcut used in examples is the "import *" variation of this syntax.

```
from sfc_models.objects import *
```

This brings in all of the objects defined in the *sfc_models.objects* module. This loads all of the "economic objects" that define models, although it currently does not include various utility classes and functions. The user needs to use "`from sfc_models.objects import *`" instead of "`from sfc_models import *`" (which would be more standard) as I had difficulties with circular import statements. (I may be able to fix that, allowing the standard syntax to work as well.)

Experienced programmers dislike the "import *" version, as it is unclear what is being imported. Imported objects might use the same name as other objects that are defined in the file. In the case of *sfc_models*, it is easy to see how new sector objects will be added over time, and they could easily use the same names as used in the user's code. As a result, code may be broken because of name clashes when the *sfc_models* package is updated. For this reason, users should avoid this syntax if they are writing complicated programs that define new objects.

One technical detail about the import statement may also trip up programmers new to the language. When a module is imported for the first time, the code in the module is executed, and the objects that are defined are then available for use. Any subsequent import statements just make the name of the module available, but the code in the module is not executed because of the import. This means that an import statement is not the same thing as pasting the code found in the imported module into the calling module – which is how the `#include` statement works in the C language. This technical issue matters if you start writing your own modules, as you need to understand the side effects of importing modules.

Within my example code, you will see the unusual-looking statement:

```
from future import print_function
```

Note that the "from future" import is required to be placed as the first line in the file. (Other import statements are typically placed at the top of code files, but this is not a requirement.) This unusual import statement is needed for examples that use the `print` statement to be backward compatible to Python 2.7.

- In Python 2.7 (and earlier), the syntax is: `print 'hello!'`
- In Python 3 (and later), the syntax changed to: `print('hello!')`

By importing "print_function," I can use Python 3 syntax in examples, and it will be interpreted properly by the Python 2.7 interpreter. *(The code within sfc_models would likely be compatible with even earlier versions of Python, except the "import from the future" support for the new print syntax would not exist. The import statement and print statements would need to be fixed, but the rest of the code would probably run.)*

Finally, I refer to *packages*. Within Python, package has a technical definition: a package is a group of Python files in the same directory, and the directory has to include a special marker file named *"__init__.py"*. The *sfc_models* framework is indeed a package, as can be verified if you locate the source code. Packages can also include sub-packages; *sfc_models* includes the *gl_book* sub-package (which refers to the book *Monetary Economics* by Godley and Lavoie.) You import modules from packages by using "." notation, as seen in example code: *"import sfc_models.models"*, or *"import sfc_models.gl_book.chapter3"*. Using existing packages is straightforward if you follow the import statements in the sample code; you will need to consult the Python documentation if you wish to create your own.

Chapter 3 Model Structure

3.1 Introduction

This chapter outlines how the *sfc_models* framework is used to build stock-flow consistent models. Some introductory code samples are given, and the overall structure used within the models is given.

The core of the logic is built around tying together economic sectors, from one or more countries. The user outlines the sectors and their relationships using high-level code, and the framework determines the underlying equations once the user invokes the model-binding step.

The sectors that have been implemented in Version 1.0 are described in Section 3.6.

3.2 Example Model Code

This section gives an example of how the *sfc_models* package can be used. The code implements Model SIM, from Godley and Lavoie's *Monetary Economics*. The objective here is just to present the coding structure; an explanation of the model is found in Section 5.3.

The code is taken from the file `intro_3_02_intro.py`, which is found in the scripts subdirectory of *sfc_models.examples*. (See Section 2.2 for script installation instructions.) The entire file (excluding the copyright notice and license) is first given, and then the sections of the code will be explained.

File: intro_3_02_intro.py

```
# Step 1: Import modules
# sfc_models code objects. Using "from <module> im-
port *" is frowned upon, but I wanted to
# have less lines of code for beginners to parse.
from sfc_models.objects import *
# Quick2DPlot() - Plotting functions used by exam-
ples; relies upon matplotlib
from sfc_models.examples.Quick2DPlot import Quick-
2DPlot
```

```
# Step 1.5: set up logging
# The next line of code sets the name of the output
files based on the code file's name.
# This means that if you paste this code into a new
file, get a new log name.
register_standard_logs('output', __file__)

# Step 2: build the model objects
# Create model, which holds all entities
mod = Model()
# Create first country - Canada. (This model only
has one country.)
can = Country(mod, 'CA', 'Canada')
# Create sectors
gov = ConsolidatedGovernment(can, 'GOV', 'Govern-
ment')
hh = Household(can, 'HH', 'Household')
# A literally non-profit business sector
bus = FixedMarginBusiness(can, 'BUS', 'Business
Sector', profit_margin=0.0)
# Create the linkages between sectors - tax flow,
markets - labour ('LAB'), goods ('GOOD')
tax = TaxFlow(can, 'TF', 'TaxFlow', .2)
labour = Market(can, 'LAB', 'Labour market')
goods = Market(can, 'GOOD', 'Goods market')
# Need to set the exogenous variable - Government
demand for Goods ("G" in economist symbology)
mod.AddExogenous('GOV', 'DEM_GOOD', '[20.,] * 105')
# Step 3: Invoke the method ("main") that builds
the model.
mod.main()

# Once the framework has built and solved the model
equations, we can either work with the output files,
# or within Python. Here, we do a plot with Quick-
2DPlot.
mod.TimeSeriesCutoff = 20
time = mod.GetTimeSeries('k')
```

```
Y_SIM = mod.GetTimeSeries('GOOD__SUP_GOOD')
Quick2DPlot(time, Y_SIM, 'Output (Y) - Model SIM',
filename='intro_3_02_Y.png')
```

When this code is run, it creates three forms of output. (As discussed later in this section, there is a potential fourth output.) The code assumes that there is a subdirectory named "output" below the directory where the file `intro_3_02_intro.py` is located.

1. Diagnostic information and the system equations are saved in the file `intro_3_02_example_log.txt`.
2. The time series output is saved in a tab-delimited text file `intro_3_02_example_out.txt`. (A tab-delimited text file is a table of text and numbers, like a spreadsheet worksheet, in which the table entries are separated by tab characters. These files are easily read by most analysis packages as well as spreadsheets. This is roughly the same thing as a csv file, but the file does not use commas to separate entries.)
3. Assuming the *matplotlib* Python package is installed, the following figure is displayed on the screen. (This figure is created by the `Quick2DPlot` call.)

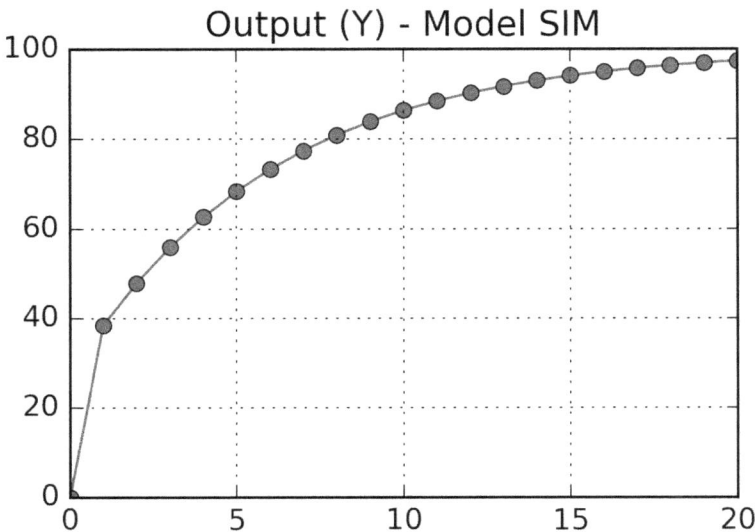

Output (Y) - Model SIM

(If the *matplotlib* library is not installed, the call to `Quick2DPlot` will just result in warning messages being displayed on the Python console. The user would need to use other software to plot the data in the tab-delimited text file.)

We will now look at the various code segments in this file. (I have removed most comments from the segments below.)

```
# Step 1: Import modules
import os
from sfc_models.models import Model, Country, Market
from sfc_models.sectors import Household,
DoNothingGovernment, TaxFlow, FixedMarginBusiness
from sfc_models.examples.Quick2DPlot import Quick2DPlot
```

The code starts by importing other modules or packages. See Section 2.7 for a longer discussion of the import statement.

The next step ("step 1.5") adds logging support).

```
register_standard_logs('output', __file__)
```

This instructs the system to create log files in the "output" subdirectory. This subdirectory is assumed to exist, and is below the directory where the Python interpreter is running, which is usually where the script is located. The user can replace this with an alternate directory. The second parameter is the base file name used for the log files. The built-in variable *__file__* is used, which is the filename of the currently running Python module (in this case, "intro_3_02_intro.py"). This idiom is used as it means that if we copy the code into a new module, the log file names will be based on the new module (and not overwrite existing files). The logging support is described in Section 3.3; for now, the user can just look at the files created in the "output" subdirectory.

The next section of the code uses the imported definitions to set up the model.

```
# Step 2: build the model objects
mod = Model()
can = Country(mod, 'CA', 'Canada')
gov = ConsolidatedGovernment(can, 'GOV',
```

```
'Government')
hh = Household(can, 'HH', 'Household')

bus = FixedMarginBusiness(can, 'BUS', 'Business
Sector', profit_margin=0.0)
tax = TaxFlow(can, 'TF', 'TaxFlow', .2)
labour = Market(can, 'LAB', 'Labour market')
goods = Market(can, 'GOOD', 'Goods market')
```

Section 3.4 discusses the object model structure used by *sfc_models*. For now, we just want to note that we create objects by calling their *constructor* functions. For example,

```
mod=Model()
```

creates a *Model* object, and assigns it to the variable *mod*. In this case, the constructor function has no arguments.

The other constructor functions that appear here have arguments. For example,

```
can = Country(mod, 'CA', 'Canada')
```

creates a *Country* object, and assigns it to the variable *can*. The first parameter to the constructor is the Model object *mod*, as the *Country* object is a child object of a *Model*; it does not exist in a vacuum. The remaining two parameters are descriptive; they give the long name of the country ("Canada"), and the short code used in equation identification ("CA").

The remaining objects are "sectors" of the Canadian economy; as can be seen, the first variable passed into the constructors is the country object they are embedded within. (As discussed in Section 3.6, the *sfc_models* framework includes other concepts as being "Sectors" of the economy, including Markets and tax flows.)

The final part of the model specification is to set the value of exogenous variables (variables that are determined outside the model equations). In this case, the only exogenous variable is government spending.

```
mod.AddExogenous('GOV', 'DEM_GOOD', '[20.,] * 105')
```

This line sets the government demand for goods ("DEM_GOOD"). This is specified as a string, and the string is an expression that can be evaluated to a Python list variable, which is treated as a time series. In this case, the government demand for goods is set at a constant $20 for 105 entries. This could be specified by writing:

```
[20., 20., 20., {...} 20.]
```

with "20." repeated 105 times. However, it is easier to use the Python idiom "[20.,] * 105" which is equivalent to:

- Create a list object with a single entry of *20.0* (written as [20.,]).
- Create a new list by copying that original list 105 times, and merging into a single list (the "*105" operation).

Additionally, my code uses "20." instead of "20"; this not just a question of taste. If I write:

```
x = 20
```

this creates a variable *x* that has the integer 20 assigned to it. (Integers have the type *int* in Python.) Whereas, if I write:

```
x = 20.
```

I am assigning the floating point number 20.000 to the variable *x*. The difference between a *float* and an *int* is obvious if I have a floating-point number with a fractional component (for example, "2.1"), but we also need to deal with floats that are also whole numbers. We could write "20.0", but Python allows us to use "20." as a shorthand. In some cases, it might be safe to mix integers with floating-point variables, but I do not recommend doing so within the *sfc_models* framework. There is code that validates inputs, and if the code is looking for a *float*, it will reject inputs that are *int*.

We are now moving on to the key processing step.

```
mod.main()
```

The third line is an invocation of the *main* method in the *mod* variable. This method is called *main* as a result of programming tradition, but it could also have been called *BuildAndSolveModel()*.

The *main()* method looks at all of the sectors that comprise the model, and ties all of the sector equations into a single block of equations. Those equations are solved (to the extent that is possible), and then the outputs are written to the log files in the "output" subdirectory.

The final (optional) block of code generates the graph shown earlier.

```
mod.TimeSeriesCutoff = 20
```

```
time = mod.GetTimeSeries('k')
Y_SIM = mod.GetTimeSeries('GOOD__SUP_GOOD')
Quick2DPlot(time, Y_SIM, 'Output (Y) - Model SIM',
filename='intro_3_02_Y.png')
```

The model's *TimeSeriesCutoff* data member is set to 20; this tells the Model object to only return the first 21 data points (0 to 21) of time series. The time axis is then extracted, using the *GetTimeSeries* method; the built-in discrete-time time axis variable is always labelled "*k*." The time axis runs from *k=0* until the end of the simulation time frame (data member *MaxTime*, default is 100). Since we set the cut-off at 20, the variable returned ends then. The model's equivalent to GDP (normally denoted *Y*) is then requested; the variable name is "GOOD__SUP_GOOD." (The naming convention is discussed in Section 3.5; in this case, it refers to the supply of goods in the goods market.) The function `Quick2DPlot` generates the graph. `Quick2DPlot` uses the *matplotlib* module, which is an external mathematical and plotting package. If *matplotlib* is not installed, `Quick2DPlot` will just print out a warning message.

3.3 How to Follow Framework Operations

If we know that the model is set up as desired, it is possible to use the output time series in Python to generate our desired output (such as a graph, or to export to a tab-delimited text file). However, it can be difficult to tell whether the model is implementing the desired behaviour without being able to browse the entire set of time series generated during simulation. Furthermore, it is possible that error messages are generated, and so it will be necessary to debug the model.

The *sfc_models* framework generates considerable diagnostic information that can be used to analyse the model operation. Additionally, a graphical model runner (which is in a preliminary state) offers a straightforward way to browse the model state, and even to step through the model binding operation.

Several log files are optionally generated. Each has an associated internal code and standard file extension. The file extension is added after a base name that is specified by the user (discussed further below). The logs are as follows.

- **[log]** (Extension: "_log.txt.") This log file is filled with messages in response to framework operations, at a low level. This file would probably be the main file used for debugging programming issues.

- **[timeseries]** (Extension: "_out.txt.") This file is a tab-delimited text file containing the time series calculated by the framework. It is suitable for viewing in a spreadsheet, or importation into another software package.
- **[eqn]** (Extension: "_eqn.txt.") A text file listing all of the equations generated by the framework.
- **[step]** (Extension: "_iteration.txt") This file is only generated if the user wishes to see the operation of the iterative solver. It outputs the value of selected variables during each step of the algorithm, and the user can then examine the output to see which variables are not converging. Since these files are large, and there can be hundreds of time steps, the solver only generates the file for a selected time step, which is specified by setting the `TraceStep` parameter in a model's EquationSolver object. For example, `model.EquationSolver.TraceStep = 5`. Since it is possible that the system will only have convergence problems at some time points, the step chosen needs to be configurable.
- **[steadystate_0]** (Extension = "_steadystate.txt.") If the user wishes to calculate an initial steady state (Section 4.5), the values of the time series in negative time is output here. (The initial steady state is calculated by starting at a negative time, and then testing whether it reaches a steady state by time zero.) If a steady state is not found, the user can examine the time series to see which did not converge.

The `Logger` class in the `sfc_models.utils` module is used to control logging at a low level. There is a convenience function in *utils*, `register_standard_logs`, that sets up the standard logs. It has two parameters: the target directory, and the base file name. An example usage is:

```
import sfc_models.utils
utils.register_standard_logs('output', __file__)
```

The above usage (common in example code) is to use the `__file__` variable as the base name for files. The `__file__` variable in Python gives the full path of the current file. The above code will generate the logs in the "output" subdirectory, and use the base name of the calling Python file. For example, if the file is "foo.py", the base will be "foo." With the base set, the log files append the extensions above. If we did use "foo.py," the log file would be "foo_log.txt."

The easier-to-use option for watching model operations is to use the *sfc_gui* graphical model runner. This is another package, found at https://github.com/brianr747/sfc_gui.

The current capabilities of the model runner allow the user to choose a Python file that generates a model. The Python files that work with the model runner have to follow a particular format; they have to have a function that generates the Model object (without calling main()). The model runner examines the structure of the Model object, and uses the embedded information to allow the user to examine the model in a graphical user interface.

- It is possible to examine the sector equation structures, both before and after model binding (calling main()).
- The model binding operation can be run one sector at a time, in order to make it clear how sector equations are being generated at the sector level.
- The equation lists can be examined.
- Economic time series can be plotted (using a very basic plotting interface). Moreover, it is possible to examine the time series during the initial steady state calculation, as well as during the iterations during a time step. Using these plots, it is usually easy to spot series that are causing convergence problems.

At the time of writing, the graphical user interface is less well supported. It is highly likely that there may be difficulties running the graphical user interface across different operating systems. Graphics capabilities are quite distinct across operating systems, whereas, the calculations within *sfc_models* should run on any Python-supported operating system. As a result, the graphics interface has been excluded from the *sfc_models* package: the standard is that the *sfc_models* package should always work on any properly installed Python interpreter (version 2.7 and beyond).

3.4 Economic Object Structure

Models are constructed by putting together objects within a hierarchy. The `Model` class organises all objects, and then methods are invoked to build and solve the mathematical model. It is possible to construct multiple `Model` objects within the same program; each runs independently of the other. All of the classes discussed in this section are subclasses of the `EconomicObject` class.

The structural hierarchy works as follows.

- The user must first create a `Model` object.
- Then, at least one `Country` object must be created, and embedded in the `Model` object. A Country must have a code, which does not contain the '_' character. Furthermore, this code must be unique within a `Model`. It is assumed that only a single currency is used within a Country object, which is specified by a currency code. If the currency code is not specified in the construction of the object, the default value equals the country code.
- Then, the user creates objects that are subclasses of `Sector` objects (such as `Household`, `Market`, `ConsolidatedGovernment`, etc.), which are embedded in a `Country` object. (For simplicity, this text will typically refer to these as 'Sector' objects, although they are technically subclasses.) Each sector must have a code assigned to it when constructed, which is unique for that `Country`. (The same sector code may be used in another country.)

The next diagram shows the layout of a multi-country model.

- All of the economic objects reside in a `Model`.
- There are three `Country` objects: CORE, PERI (for periphery), and US. CORE and PERI share a currency (EUR), while the US uses USD.
- The framework automatically created two `CurrencyZone` objects, which encompass the `Country` objects that share the same currency code. The user never directly creates these objects, and embeds the `Country` object directly into the model (and not the `CurrencyZone`); the dashed lines indicate

`CurrencyZone`'s special status.

- Finally, each Country has one or more sector objects embedded within them.

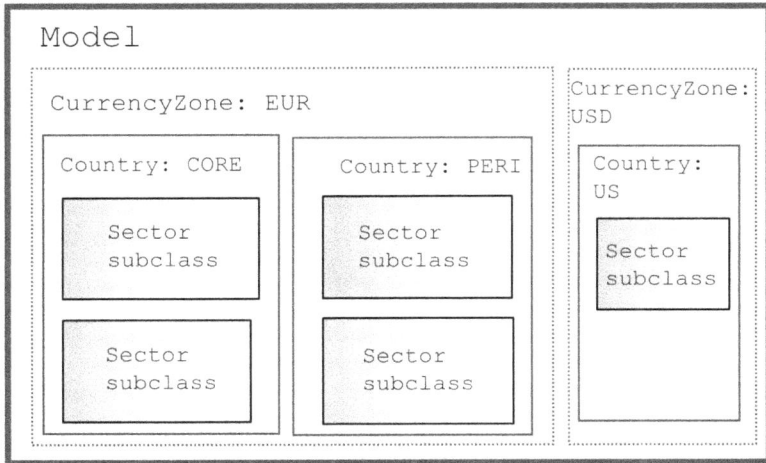

All of these types of objects – `Model`, `Country`, and `Sector` – are subclasses of the `EconomicObject` class. The `EconomicObject` class is used to track the hierarchy of these objects, and assigns each of these code objects a unique integer ID. This ID is used internally to distinguish objects, and it appears in logs.

The name `Country` could be viewed as somewhat misleading as these objects do not have to correspond to a single nation-state. They are really just a grouping of sectors that share a common currency. We can handle situations that are more complicated as follows.

- A `Country` can stand for multiple nation-states that share a currency.
- A single nation-state can be decomposed into multiple `Country` objects that share the same currency. For example, Canadian provinces could be examined in this way.
- A single nation-state in which two currencies are used in commerce could be composed of several '`Country`' objects, with differing currencies. National economic aggregates would re-

quire aggregating across these components. (The alternative – allowing `Sector` objects to have accounting entries in multiple currencies – would be far more complex and error-prone.)

The framework defines a `Region` class that is a subclass of `Country`, which may be used if users are distressed by referring to entities like provinces as `Country` objects. The only distinction between the `Region` and `Country` classes is that the `Region` class uses the `DefaultCurrency` data member of the `Model` object to set its currency code. (The `DefaultCurrency` starts as 'LOC', and then switches to the currency code of the last `Country` object defined.) This means that if we define several `Region` objects (without specifying their currency in construction), they will all share the same currency. However, they are otherwise identical to `Country` objects for framework operations. Chapter 6 discusses multi-country models in more detail.

The bulk of the computer operations involve sector objects. These objects contain almost all of the equations that define the mathematical model that is generated. (The `Model` object may contain global equations that are defined by the user, and it contains information on adjustments made to the sector equations.) The types of sector objects available in Version 1.0 of *sfc_models* are described in Section 3.6. More sector types will be created either by additions to the *sfc_models*, or by extensions to the framework (as described in Chapter 7).

It should be noted that although these classes are derived from the `Sector` class, they do not necessarily correspond to economic sectors as normally defined in the national accounts. We may also insert other classes that act to bind together the true economic sectors.

- The `Market` class ties together sectors that supply and demand the same good or service. These may correspond to financial markets (such as the international gold market), or the notional labour market.
- The `TaxFlow` class determines the flow of taxes between the appropriate sectors within a `CurrencyZone` or `Country`. This is kept as a separate object from the governmental sectors so that it is easier to switch out the code that determines taxes.

The order of the creation of `Sector` objects should not matter; all that is required is that they are constructed after their containing `Coun-`

`try`. The objective is that it is possible to construct a model with any combination of `Sectors`, and examine the resulting equations. (There is no guarantee that there will be a solution, however. For example, many models will not have solutions unless there is a positive tax rate to damp down income growth.) However, this objective was not entirely met at the time of writing – some `Sector` classes assume that other `Sector` classes were also created in the same `Country` – and so model binding (described next) will fail if those other sectors have not been created before binding. These dependencies should be removed over time.

The step of *model binding* normally occurs when we call the `main()` method of the `Model` object. (The `main()` method is composed of multiple steps, which may be decomposed when running models in the graphical user interface.) Until binding occurs, the `Model` state is "Construction," and the user is able to keep inserting new objects or information (initial conditions, etc.) Binding the model ties all of the economic objects together, which leads to the `Model` generating a final set of mathematical equations that are to be solved.

Within a `Country`, `Sector` objects are distinguished by their code. These codes become components of Python variable names, and so have to follow rules that govern variable names: no whitespace characters (spaces, tabs), most symbols ("*", "/", etc.), and an internal requirement: no underscore ("_") characters. (The requirements for `Country` and currency codes are similar, and for the same reason.)

The sector code (data member Code) is not enough to specify fully a sector within a model; the FullCode needs to be used. The FullCode is defined as follows.

- If there is a single `Country` object in the `Model`, the `FullCode` equals the sector `Code`.
- If there are multiple `Country` objects, the FullCode equals "{country.Code}_{sector.Code}"; that is, the code of the containing `Country` and the code of the sector, separated by an underscore. For example, if a `Household` sector has code 'HH,' and is in a Country with code 'CA,' the FullCode is 'CA_HH.' The reason why we do not allow underscores in sector/country codes is that the presence of the underscore distinguishes a FullCode from a Code in a multi-country environment.

Although code structure would be simpler if the code from the `Country` was always prepended to the sector code, that makes the variable names unnecessarily long in single-country models. The complexity in the current system is that we may not know whether it is a multi-country model until the model is finally bound together, and so we have to be careful when working with the FullCode ahead of the binding step.

3.5 Variables and Equations

The structure of the equations within the *sfc_models* framework is described in greater length in Chapter 4. The binding together of the economic objects leads to the creation of a block of equations, which are then solved by an `EquationSolver`. The current structure of the solver is that each variable is defined by a single equation, which may involve any number of other variables (including zero other variables).

In the final set of equations, their structure is of the following form:

variable_name = equation_associated_with_variable.

As will be seen, the full names of variables can be quite long, and they will vary depending on the model structure. The key simplification is that the equations associated with variables in a given sector refer to other variables within that sector, and we can use a more useful short name for that variable.

The full name of the variable is equal to the FullCode of the `Sector` object containing the variable, two underscores ('__'), and then the short name of the variable. For example, imagine if we had the following situation:

- There is a Sector object with Code "YY" (assigned to variable `sector_yy`), with a local variable named `Y` that equals two times another local variable `W`.
- There is a second sector, with Code "XX" (assigned to `sector_xx`), with a local variable named X, which equals the previous sector's local variable `Y` plus 2.0.

The equation defining `Y` within Sector "YY" (`sectory_yy`) is straightforward:

```
Y = 2*W
```

That is, we can define `Y` solely by using the local variable name. Note that we typically implement such an equation by breaking it into components, using the `AddVariable()` method. In this case, the code would look like:

```
sector_yy.AddVariable('Y', 'Equation defining Y',
'2*W')
```

As can be seen, the arguments are all string variables. The first string is the name of the variable, the second is a description of the equation, and the third is a string of Python code that would be evaluated to determine the value of the variable.

Defining the variable X in Sector "XX" is more complicated. It cannot refer to the name of the variable in the other sector by its local name (Y). Instead, it needs to get the full name of the variable from sector_yy, and use that within the defining equation. The following code sample demonstrates how this is done.

File: intro_3_05_variable_names_1.py.

```
from __future__ import print_function

import sfc_models
from sfc_models.models import Model, Country
from sfc_models.sector import Sector

mod = Model()
can = Country(mod, 'CA', 'Canada')
# has_F=False: turns off creation of financial asset
variables.
sector_yy = Sector(can, 'YY', has_F=False)
sector_yy.AddVariable('W', 'Variable W <constant>',
'4.0')
sector_yy.AddVariable('Y', 'Variable Y - depends on
local variable', '2*W')

sector_xx = Sector(can, 'XX', has_F=False)
variable_name = sector_yy.GetVariableName('Y')
# format: inserts variable_name where {0} is
eqn = '{0} + 2.0'.format(variable_name)
sector_xx.AddVariable('X', 'Variable x; depends on
other sector', eqn)
# Bind the model; solve
eqns = mod.main()
print(eqns)
```

The text equations returned from `mod.main()` include (there are some extra lines which we ignore here):

```
YY__W = 4.0          # [W] Variable W <constant>
YY__Y = 2 *YY__W     # [Y] Variable Y - depends on
local variable
XX__X = YY__Y +2.0   # [X] Variable x; depends on
other sector
```

If we modify the code slightly by putting sector_xx into a different country, the final equations are modified.

File: intro_3_05_variable_names_2.py

```
from __future__ import print_function

import sfc_models
from sfc_models.models import Model, Country
from sfc_models.sector import Sector

mod = Model()
can = Country(mod, 'CA', 'Canada')
# has_F=False: turns off creation of financial asset
variables.
sector_yy = Sector(can, 'YY', has_F=False)
sector_yy.AddVariable('W', 'Variable W <constant>',
'4.0')
sector_yy.AddVariable('Y', 'Variable Y - depends on
local variable', '2*W')
# Only the next two lines have changed: put sector_
xx into a another Country
us = Country(mod, 'US')
sector_xx = Sector(us, 'XX', has_F=False)
variable_name = sector_yy.GetVariableName('Y')
# format: inserts variable_name where {0} is
eqn = '{0} + 2.0'.format(variable_name)
sector_xx.AddVariable('X', 'Variable x; depends on
other sector', eqn)
# Bind the model; solve
eqns = mod.main()
print(eqns)
```

```
The equation output:
CA_YY__W = 4.0                   # [W] <...>
CA_YY__Y = 2 *CA_YY__W           # [Y] <...>
US_XX__X = CA_YY__Y +2.0         # [X] <...>
```

- In both cases, the FullCode is prepended to all variable names in the final result. The names include the country code (CA_YY__Y) in the two-country model, whereas they are just the sector code (YY__Y) in the single-country mode.
- The definition of the equation for variable Y was easy, as it just referred to local variables.
- Since the variable name changes, the equation for variable X in sector_xx needed to use the method GetVariableName to get the variable name safely.

The variable name returned by GetVariableName depends upon whether we are in the construction phase.

```
Name of variable before binding: _3__Y
Variable name after binding: CA_YY__Y
```

Before binding, we do not know the FullCode of a sector (since the framework is unaware whether we are in a multi-country model). Therefore, GetVariableName returns an alias to the variable name. These aliases are replaced during the model building process within main(). After the model is bound, the FullCode is known, and GetVariableName returns the final name used within the equation block.

This technique needs to be used when extending *sfc_models* (Chapter 7), and creating cross-sector linkages in equations.

3.6 Sector Definitions

The economic logic of the sfc_models package is mainly implemented in the subclasses of the Sector class; the rest of the framework acts to support these classes. The idea is that it is now quite easy to add new economic functionality, using the existing sector classes as their starting point. For most researchers, that would be the primary area of interest.

Most sector definitions that are built into the *sfc_models* package are included in the sfc_models.sector_definitions module. That is, if you want to work with the Household sector, you would use the following `import` statement.

```
from sfc_models.sector_definitions import Household
```

The Market class is an exception to the placement in sector_definitions; it is currently found in sfc_models.sector along with the base Sector class. You can import all of these objects by using:

```
from sfc_models.objects import *
```

If you examine the `sfc_models.sector_definitions` module, you will find many subclasses of the `Sector` class. Not all of them are meant to be incorporated into models; they are abstract base classes. One example is the `BaseHousehold`, which is the parent of all of the various household sector classes. These classes are only of interest for developers creating new classes, and so they are not discussed herein. (Those developers are directed to the internal code documentation.)

There are two types of sector classes within the framework.

1. Classes that implement economic sectors, as they are normally understood within the national accounts (and the academic SFC models literature).

2. Classes that implement the linkages between the sectors that are economic sectors. These linkage sectors do not hold financial assets, and so are missing the associated balance sheet and flow equations.

These subclasses all have two key methods:

1. the constructor (named `__init__` in Python), which includes parameters used to define sector behaviour; and

2. the `_GenerateEquations()` method, which is called during the model binding step to fill in equations. (The method has a leading underscore to hide it from the help command – this is a method that is called by the framework, and not the user.)

The constructor is called when an object is created. For these subclasses, the usual behaviour is to call the constructor of the class's parent, and then store parameters as data members in the class. Some variables will be defined, but only the equations that are guaranteed to be unchanged by interactions with other sectors can be filled in.

The `_GenerateEquations()` method does most of the work. It is only called after all sectors have been included in the model, and so it is possible for the method to start looking for other sectors to interact with. Even equations with parameters (should) be filled in here, as it is possible that the user may wish to set the value of the parameter in code outside the constructor.

Chapter 5 and 6 will discuss how models are built using these sectors. The remainder of this section outlines the built-in sectors, and the parameters used to define their behaviour.

We will start with the `Household` sector. Since how objects are created may not be obvious to those who are new to object-oriented programming, the explanation will be more detailed than the following sectors, as they typically follow the pattern of this sector.

Household. The `Household` sector is a key sector, as it provides both a labour output (default code LAB), and it is the major source of demand for goods (default code: GOOD). The Household object constructor is as follows.

```
hh = Household(country, code, long_name='', al-
pha_income=0.6, alpha_fin=0.4, consumption_good_
name='GOOD', labour_name='LAB')
```

The syntax `hh = Household()` is an example of calling a constructor. The call constructs a `Household` object, which is assigned to the variable `hh`. The constructor is implemented in the special method called `__init__` in all classes. If you look at the class definitions in code, the `__init__` method has an additional argument at the front of the list, normally called `self`. The variable `self` refers to the object being constructed, which is assigned to the variable `hh`.

The first two arguments (country, code), are required parameters for the construction of all sectors. The first (country) is the Country object into which this `Sector` is being embedded. The second is the sector code, which is a string that meets the requirements described in Section 3.4. (No symbols, underscores, must be unique to the `Country`.)

The following arguments of the form variable=default are optional parameters. (If they are not specified, the default value is used.) Such default parameters may appear in any Python function or method, and not just constructors.

- If the user does not specify the names of the variables when calling the method, they have to be supplied in the order specified in the method.

- If user specifies the variable names, they can be supplied in any order, so long as this is done after the non-named variables are listed. This allows you to skip over arguments with default parameters.

For example, the two following calls are equivalent to each other.

```
hh = Household(ca, 'HH', 'Household')
```

or

```
hh = Household(ca, 'HH', long_name='Household')
```

These first three parameters are the same for all `Sector` subclasses. The `long_name` is a user-supplied longer description of the `Sector`. It has limited usefulness at present, although it may show up more if model construction migrates to a graphical user interface.

The remaining optional parameters are specific to the Household sector (although some other subclasses inherit from Household, and they share these parameters).

- `alpha_income` (default is 0.6). This is the propensity to consume out of income. This means that if it is 0.6, 60% of that income is spent on consumption goods (with the good name specified below).
- `alpha_fin` (default is 0.4). The propensity to consume out of financial wealth (denoted F in this package).
- `consumption_good_name` (default is 'GOOD'). The `Houshold` acts as a source of demand for the good with code specified by this parameter. Normally, there is no need to change the default, but this may need to be done in sectors with more than one `Household` sector within a `Country`.
- `labour_name` (default is 'LAB.'). This is the code of the type of labour output supplied by this sector. Most readers may be surprised to find out that there is no upper limit to the amount of labour that can be supplied. This is described in Section 5.3.

Capitalists. The `Capitalists` sector is similar to the `House-hold` sector, but it does not supply labour. It will instead receive dividends from a business sector object, with the inflow assigned to the variable DIV.

```
cap = Capitalists(country, code, long_name='', al-
pha_income=.7, alpha_fin=.3,consumption_good_name='GOOD')
```

The parameters are the same as the Household sector (except it is missing `labour_name`).

- `alpha_income` (default is 0.7). Propensity to consume out of income.
- `alpha_fin` (default is 0.3). Propensity to consume out of financial assets.
- `consumption_good_name` (default is 'GOOD'). Target of consumption.

HouseholdWithExpectations. The `HouseholdWithExpectations` sector is similar to the Household sector, except that its consumption is based on "expected income." This is implemented as adaptive expectations – the previous period's income is used to predict the present. The implementation of expectations is discussed in Section 5.4.

```
hh_e = HouseholdWithExpectations(country, code,
long_name='', alpha_income=.7, alpha_fin=.3, consump-
tion_good_name='GOOD', labour_name='LAB')
```

The same parameters as the Household sector once again.

- `alpha_income` (default is 0.7). Propensity to consume out of income.
- `alpha_fin` (default is 0.3). Propensity to consume out of financial assets.
- `consumption_good_name` (default is 'GOOD'). Target of consumption.
- `labour_name` (default is 'LAB'). Code for the labour market used.

FixedMarginBusiness. The `FixedMarginBusiness` offers simplified business sector dynamics. The profit margin is specified, and the business is guaranteed to receive that margin on total output. It adjusts its labour demand so that it always hires enough workers to meet the demand for its output. In other words, it can perfectly predict demand for its output within the current period. There is no notion of capital in this sector, and production is linear: if you double labour input, output doubles. Furthermore, it is assumed that it is selling into a single market. (The Fixed-MarginBusinessMultiOutput class is a subclass of this sector that relaxes that assumption; described later.)

Businesses do not pay taxes on profits (which is unintentionally realistic). If a `Capitalists` sector exists within the same `Country`, all profits will be paid to that sector. (There is currently no support for allowing multiple sector ownership, out-of-country owners, or multiple allowing `Capitalists` sectors in the same `Country`.)

The simplifying assumptions are relaxed in more advanced stock-flow consistent models in the academic literature (including Godley and Lavoie's Monetary Economics). For example, if we want to relax the assumption that the business sector always perfectly predicts demand in the current period, we need to model inventories.

```
bus = FixedMarginBusiness(country, code, long_
name='', profit_margin=0.0, labour_input_name='LAB',
output_name='GOOD')
```

Optional parameters:

- `profit_margin` (default = 0.0). Guaranteed profit margin out of revenue. For example, if 0.1, guarantees a 10% profit margin (or labour cost is 90% of total revenue).
- `labour_input_name` (default='LAB'). The source of demand for the labour market.
- `output_name` (default= 'GOOD'). The single output of this sector.

ConsolidatedGovernment. The `ConsolidatedGovernment` class is the simplest implementation of the government sector within sfc_models. It is the result of consolidating the central bank (which implements monetary policy) with the Treasury (which implements fiscal policy). The central government is the default issuer of money and government deposits.

```
gov = ConsolidatedGovernment(country, code, long_
name='')
```

There are no optional parameters (other than `long_name`). This reflects the fact that the consolidated government does little by default; fiscal policy is implemented by setting the tax rate (in a separate Tax-

`Flow` object, described below), and government spending (consumption) is assumed to be set as an exogenous variable. The lack of behaviour is reflected in the name of the `DoNothingGovernment` class, which is an alias of the `ConsolidatedGovernment` class.

TaxFlow. The `TaxFlow` class encapsulates the calculations used for taxation. It is not a true economic sector, rather a support object. It handles the taxation within a single `Country`. The creation syntax is:

```
Taxflow = TaxFlow(country, code, long_name='',
taxrate=0.0, taxes_paid_to='GOV')
```

Optional parameters:

- `taxrate`: The rate of taxation, between 0 and 1. The assumption is that all tax-paying sectors pay taxes at a flat percentage of gross income.
- `taxes_paid_to`: The sector that receives the tax flow, typically either a `ConsolidatedGovernment` or `Treasury` object.

`TaxFlow` objects generate the terms associated with tax payments during model binding. The behaviour is as follows.

1. Cycle through all other `Sector` objects within the same `Country`.
2. If the object's `IsTaxable` member is set to `False`, it skips over to the next object. At present, only the classes derived from `BaseHousehold` are marked as taxable; however, the user could allow for the business sector to pay taxes by setting the `IsTaxable` member variable to `True`.
3. If the object has a `TaxRate` variable defined, it uses that variable within calculations. Otherwise, it uses the `TaxFlow`'s `TaxRate` variable, which is the default tax rate for the `Country`.
4. Within the other sector, it creates the variable T, which is the taxes paid. It adds the other (taxpaying) sector's tax payment to the list of terms within the total taxes variable within the `TaxFlow` object (also labelled T).
5. Finally, once all sectors are processed, the sector that is the recipient of the taxes (the central government) is given a cash

flow that is equal to the total tax variable within the `TaxFlow` object.

Although it may have been more intuitive to have the taxation operations embedded within the government object, this would have created undesirable complexity. The rules for setting tax rates would be associated with particular implementations of central government spending. (For example, we could create a central government that operates a welfare state, and spending would no longer be exogenous, but rather depend on the state of the business cycle.) By splitting the taxation rules into a separate object, we have decoupled the two sides of fiscal policy, and it is easier to modify them independently.

There are many extensions of `TaxFlow` behaviour possible. Value-added taxes that depend upon spending, tariffs, business sector taxation, or emulating progressive income taxes would be of interest.

Treasury. The `Treasury` class is the fiscal arm of the central government in the case where the role of the government has been split into two areas: monetary and fiscal. Like the `ConsolidatedGovernment`, it currently has a minimal implementation (as spending is an exogenous variable in the models covered). It would become more complex if spending depends upon the state of the economy (which would be the case for simulating a welfare state). The Treasury is the default issuer of (government) deposits, which are effectively the same as Treasury bills for most purposes.

Once again, there are no optional parameters in the object construction (other than long_name):

```
tre = Treasury(country, code, long_name='')
```

CentralBank. The `CentralBank` object is the supplier of money in models with a disaggregated government. It buys government deposits (issued by the `Treasury`) which pay interest, and issues money (with an interest rate of 0%). Under the assumption that deposit rates are not negative, it will generate profits based on the interest rate spread. It pays a dividend to the `Treasury` based on those profits.

The object creation

```
cb = CentralBank(country, code, long_name='',
treasury=None)
```

Optional parameter:

- `treasury`. If the Treasury object has been created, it can be passed into the constructor; it will be assigned to the member variable `self.Treasury`. Otherwise, the `Treasury` member variable will need to be set within the `CentralBank` object before model binding.

At model binding, the central bank will add a cash flow from itself to the sector set as the member variable `Treasury`. The default behaviour is that all interest received is paid to the Treasury as a dividend.

Market. The `Market` class is a support class that manages the market interactions between other sectors. It is an important base class, and its source code is found in `sfc_models.sector`.

There are no optional parameters during creation.

```
market_obj = Market(self, country, code,
long_name='')
```

The code associated with a market is the code name for the "commodity" being traded in the market, and is critical for its implementation. (The commodity could be a good or service; and for the `FinancialAssetMarket` subclass, financial asset markets.) During model binding, the Market object looks for sectors within the same country that have a demand for the commodity with that that code. (Note that it is possible to have a supplier from outside the same country, but demand is always local. The demand for the commodity is denoted by creating a variable with the prefix "DEM_" in the sector. (For example, if the commodity code is "GOODS," one adds a "DEM_GOODS" variable to the sector.)

Demand is measured as a currency (for example, dollar) amount, not quantity. This keeps the variable in the same units as the other flow variables within the framework. At the time of writing, there is no support for quantity or price variables associated with `Market` objects. However, once this support is added, it will be an average price for all quantities traded during the period (see Section 3.7).

The behaviour of the supply side is more complex. There are three possible ways supply can be handled.

1. The user does not explicitly set a sector as being a supplier. In this case, the Market object searches the Country for a single

sector that has a supply variable associated with the market (a variable named "SUP_{code}."

2. The user specifies a single supplier using the AddSupplier method. The supplier does not have to be from within the same country. This explicit setting of a supplier is needed for models with cross-country trade flows. The user will also need to create an ExternalSector object in this case, as discussed in Chapter 6. The assumption is that the supplier has the capacity (and willingness) to supply all that is demanded by the demand sectors. The possibility of supply limitations would have to be added in later extensions. This base functionality implies that the economy is entirely demand-led; there are no supply side limitations.

3. The user creates multiple suppliers using the `AddSupplier` method. In this case, the user needs to specify how demand is allocated among the various suppliers. The assumption is that if there are N supplying sectors, the user specifies a supply allocation for N-*1* of those sectors, and the remaining sector is the residual sector that supplies the remaining demand. For example, if there is a domestic and foreign supply sector of consumer goods within the country, the supply allocated to the foreign supplier is given by the propensity to import, and the domestic supplier supplies the rest.

The syntax to set a non-residual supplier is to call `AddSupplier` with a supply allocation term:

```
market_object.AddSupplier(supplier,
supply_eqn='{equation}')
```

FinancialAssetMarket. The `FinancialAssetMarket` class is the base class for markets in financial assets. The assumption is that for each type of financial asset, there is only a single issuer. Like the Market class, it is found in `sfc_models.sector`. The user is not normally expected to directly create such objects, rather they will create objects from subclasses (such as `DepositMarket` or `MoneyMarket`, discussed next).

DepositMarket. The `DepositMarket` class implements government-issued deposits. The default code for this object is "DEP." These deposits could be thought of as Treasury bills, except that they follow a deposit interest convention: the buyer always pays the par price for the deposit, and is paid a certain amount of interest in the following time period. The rate of interest on deposits is the variable r within the `DepositMarket` object. Since the interest is paid upon the previous period's deposit holdings, the class needs to work with the previous period's supply and demand variables. This is implemented by creating new time series with "LAG_" prepended to the variable name. For example, a sector would have a `DEM_DEP` variable (demand for deposits), and `LAG_DEM_DEP` which is equal to the `DEM_DEP` variable with a one period delay.

The constructor call for the `DepositMarket` is given by:

```
deposit_market_object = DepositMarket(country,
code='DEP', long_name='',issuer_short_code='GOV')
```

Optional parameter:
- `issuer_short_code`: Which sector issues the deposits? (The default is the default code for the ConsolidatedGovernment – GOV.)

MoneyMarket. The `MoneyMarket` handles the demand for money within the model. This is the simplest possible financial asset market, as money is assumed to pay no interest. (If it paid interest, it would be equivalent to a `DepositMarket`.)

```
money_market_object = MoneyMarket(country,
code='MON', long_name='', issuer_short_code='GOV')
```

Optional parameter.
- `issuer_short_code`: which sector issues money?

The assumption within sfc_models is that sectors in a country hold money as a residual financial asset if a `MoneyMarket` object is created within that country. If the sector does not explicitly set a demand for money ('DEM_MON'), it is assumed that it will hold all financial assets in the form of money. That is, during model binding, the `MoneyMarket` object will add a demand for money that equals the amount of financial asset holdings ("F").

FixedMarginBusinessMultiOutput. The `FixedMarginBusinessMultiOutput` class is an extension of the `FixedMarginBusiness` class. As the name suggests, it is a business sector that supplies more than one market. The main use of this class is to allow a business sector to supply both domestic markets and foreign markets. The construction syntax is as follows.

```
business = FixedMarginBusinessMultiOutput(country,
code, long_name='', profit_margin=0.0, labour_input_
name='LAB', market_list=())
```

Optional parameters:
- `profit_margin` (default = 0.0). Guaranteed profit margin out of revenue. For example, if 0.1, guarantees a 10% profit margin (or labour cost is 90% of total revenue).
- `labour_input_name` (default='LAB'). The source of demand for the labour market.
- `market_list`. A list of market objects that are supplied by this business.

A difference between this class constructor and the `FixedMargin-Business` constructor is that there is no output code, since the output of this business is associated with multiple `Market` objects. Instead, the user supplies the list of `Market` objects.

GoldStandardGovernment. The `GoldStandardGovernment` class is a subclass of ConsolidatedGovernment that implements the gold standard behavioural rules to manage the value of its currency. The government buys or sells gold in a fashion that ensures that its currency value remains fixed. The amount of gold held is tracked, but at present, there is nothing to prevent gold holdings from becoming negative. In the real world, a government would either devalue (or de-link from gold completely) before running out of gold.

The operation of the `GoldStandardGovernment` requires the creation of an `ExternalSector` object, as described in Chapter 6.

The constructor is as follows.

```
gov = GoldStandardGovernment(country, code, long_
name='', initial_gold_stock=0.0)
```

Optional parameter.
- `initial_gold_stock`: The initial gold stock in ounces.

GoldStandardCentralBank. Similar to the `GoldStandardGovernment`, the `GoldStandardCentralBank` implements the gold standard operations for the case where the government is split between a central bank and a Treasury. In this case, the central bank handles foreign exchange operations, while the Treasury undertakes only domestic transactions (and hence the original Treasury class is unchanged).

```
cb = GoldStandardCentralBank(country, code, long_
name='', treasury=None, initial_gold_stock=0.0)
```

Optional parameters.
- `treasury`. If the Treasury object has been created, it can be passed into the constructor; it will be assigned to the member variable `self.Treasury`. Otherwise, the `Treasury` member variable will need to be set within the `CentralBank` object before model binding.
- `initial_gold_stock`. The initial gold stock in ounces.

3.7 The Law of One Price

Within *sfc_models*, we make the simplification: all transactions of the same type (within the same market) occur at the same price within the same accounting period. If the household sector is buying goods from the business sector, all households pay the same price. (If one wanted, one could create a "wholesale" and "retail" market objects for the same good, and have differing retail prices. Even so, all households would see the same price.)

This simplification is standard for economic models, and so most economists are familiar with it. However, this may raise some questions by those who are less familiar with the assumption.

The assumption is arguably unrealistic; we consistently see different prices for the same good, and many prices (such as financial asset prices) change many times during the accounting period of an economic model (typically monthly or quarterly).

The interpretation is that it is a weighted average price for all transactions during the period, defined so that accounting relationships add up. This matches the data that we are typically trying to emulate: national accounting data. That is, the situation is less confusing if we think of the prices within the model as matching a price index.

Therefore, there is no requirement that the economic "law of one price" holds at the micro level; prices within the model correspond to observed macro averages. The mechanisms that would determine the exact prices for all transactions within the accounting period are assumed to be beyond the scope of the model. Furthermore, there is no presumption that we can go from "micro" behaviour to the observed macro behaviour in the model.

It is presumably possible to develop models at a lower level of aggregation that allows for multiple prices within the same accounting period. For example, agent-based modelling could allow each agent to see different prices. Such microstructure would matter for some models, such as a detailed analysis of the interactions in the financial markets, where dealers act as intermediaries between investors and issuers. Such a level of detail is well beyond the scope of most macro models (the focus of *sfc_models*).

Finally, the fact that prices are averages means that behaviour would appear different if we change the model frequency. For example, a quarterly price is an average of three monthly prices. If the price level is trending during the period, decisions by agents (sectors) may end up with different outcomes during the same three-month period (all else held equal). This would be a problem if we believed that SFC models were "true" models of the economy. However, if we accept that they are always going to be approximations to reality, this is not a concern. Similar realism issues are further discussed in Appendix A.1.

Chapter 4 Equations and Their Solution

4.1 Introduction

The bulk of this book covers the task of building a model by putting together sector objects. Although it would be nice to add more complicated
descriptions of economic behaviour, we run into a roadblock – those complicated models are useless unless we can find a solution. Therefore, we need
to understand how the equation solver works before adding new features.

The strategy chosen within the *sfc_models* framework is to decompose
model building from equation solution (although the equation solver is invoked from within the `main()` method for convenience). The equations
could be extracted from the model (for example, by writing them to a file),
and then solved using other packages. (Or by pencil and paper, if one is sufficiently masochistic.) The built-in equation solver within the package has been
good enough to solve the systems built so far, but it is hardly state-of-the-art.

The author did only a rudimentary scan of what was already available in
Python to improve the solution routines. Adding in other packages would
probably be the best way forward, but users who are more familiar with
other languages may wish to use the equation solution techniques already
available to them. The advantage of the current configuration is that there
are no true dependencies upon other packages for installation. This means
that casual users can run provided examples only after a single, easy installation step. (Since *sfc_models* is pure Python, it has fewer potential installation problems than packages that rely on non-Python libraries, which can
be the case for many of the mathematical packages.)

Finally, even if users want to switch over to a more robust equation solver,
they will need to prune the equations that are generated by the framework.
In order to be able to generate the equations algorithmically, the framework
needs to cover all possible variable assignments. The result is that there
are redundant equations that can cause difficulties for numerical solution.

4.2 Equation and EquationBlock Classes

The calculation of equations within the package is ultimately achieved by evaluating the strings that define the equations. This is unlike how such evaluations are usually done: specifying equations as being of a particular format, and then specifying the model as numerical parameters. For example, a linear model is typically specified as a set of matrices.

This creates a great deal of flexibility within the modelling framework: we can incorporate practically any nonlinear function we wish within behavioural equations. The cost is that we put a lot of pressure on the solver.

In order to get more structure within equations, the `Equation` and `EquationBlock` classes were created. They are found in the *sfc_models. equation* module.

As the name suggests, the `Equation` class implements a single equation. These equations are not completely general: the left-hand side consists of a single variable. That is *"variable_name = (right hand side of equation)."*

The `EquationBlock` acts as a holder of equation objects. They are saved in a dictionary (Python `dict`), which creates the constraint that each variable name within an equation block is unique. That is, adding an `Equation` with the same variable name as an existing `Equation` overwrites the original.

The Equation class only offers limited functionality. The key feature is the AddTerm() method, which adds a new term (something like $-x$ or $+y$) to the equation. It has a limited ability to add and cancel out terms.

The following example shows this cancellation ability.

```
from __future__ import print_function
from sfc_models.equation import Equation
eq = Equation('x=y')
print('Start:', str(eq))
eq.AddTerm('-y')
print('Final:', str(eq))
```

The output:

```
Start: x=y
Final: x=0.0
```

The other set of functionality is the ability to replace variables safely. This allows us to do things like replace aliases for variables. The key is that the equation is broken up into *tokens,* which is safer than "find and replace." For example, a standard find and replace operation on the variable `foo` will also affect `foobar`, but these are diagnosed as being distinct tokens.

Unfortunately, the `Equation` class was developed late in the development cycle, and at the time of writing is only used during the model-building steps. The final set of equations is converted to a multi-line string, and the `EquationSolver` works on the multi-line string. (One advantage of the current configuration is that it is possible to test the solver solely by inputting text strings, without needing to work with `Equation` objects.)

Since it is likely that the `Equation` class will take over much of the functionality that is embedded in the equation parsing routines in the solver, I will just direct the user to the internal documentation. Typing "`help(Equation)`" on the console (with the Equation class imported) gives up-to-date usage examples.

4.3 Solver Syntax

The `EquationSolver` class takes a block of equations and then attempts to find a solution. The equation block is assumed to have a simple structure, consisting of a list of equality statements. The `Equation-Parser` class does the parsing of the equations; the `EquationSolver` has a member named `Parser`, which is (unsurprisingly) an object of the `Parser` class.

The package uses the following two terms (standard in economics) to categorise variables: *endogenous* and *exogenous*. *Endogenous* variables are the variables that are determined by the system of equations to be solved. *Exogenous* variables are variables that are set externally to the system of equations.

The equality statements must be of the following type:

- A variable is set to be equal to some expression, which must be a Python expression. (For example, you use "`*`" for multiplication.) These are the endogenous variables.
- The initial conditions of a variable (defined earlier) is set by an expression of the form "{variable}(0) = {constant value}." For example: `x(0)  =20.0`.
- A variable can be defined to be the lagged value of another variable. This is set by an expression of the format "{lagged variable} = {target variable}(k-1)." For example: "`lag_x = x(k-1)`". (The variable *k* is reserved; it is the current time step, and always runs from 0 to the maximum time.

- There is a block of exogenous variable definitions. Exogenous variables are set using the syntax "{variable} = {Python list expression}." (The Python list expression syntax is discussed below.)

The exogenous variable definitions will override the definition of a variable if it is found within the block of endogenous variables. All exogenous variable definitions are placed at the end of the text block, following a line that includes the text "exogenous" (case insensitive). The values of an exogenous variable are specified as a Python list. This includes the following possibilities:

- Explicitly list all values. x=[1.0, 2.0, 3.0], sets x for the first three time steps.
- Use the "*" operator to get repeated values. x= [10.0,] * 20 sets x to be 10 for 20 time steps.
- Use the "+" operator to build up a list. x = [10.0,] * 5 + [20.0,]*25 sets x=10.0 for the first 5 time steps, and 20.0 for the next 25.

Exogenous variables have to be defined to be at least as long as the maximum running time of the model. If the exogenous variable is a constant, this can be achieved easily by leaving it within the block of endogenous variables, and setting it to be a constant. The only drawback is that the variable is not explicitly described as exogenous, which may reduce the ease of understanding the model.

One important fact to keep in mind is that all variables are in fact time series. For example, if a parameter such as the propensity to consume is declared as a variable, it will create an associated time series. This allows us to declare later the parameter as an exogenous variable, so that we can see the effect of changing the parameter. A parameter is only fixed (and has no time series) if it appears as a constant within the equation block. For example:

```
x = y + 1.0
y = 2.0
```

will create two variables (x, y), with associated time series. We could then replace the definition of *y* with an exogenous variable declaration, which will then affect *x*. The constant 1.0 is hard-coded into the equations.

Note that I use "1.0" instead of "1" in the equations; this is to ensure that the equation is interpreted as a float, and not an integer value. Python accepts "1." instead of "1.0", but I add the redundant ".0" here and in my examples since readers who are unfamiliar with Python may assume that is a typo.

The convention used within the equations is that we are solving at time period k, with $k>0$. (The initial time step is always at $k=0$, and is a special case, as described below.) Where variables appear within equations, it is actually a reference to its value at time k. If you want to translate the equations that appear within the equation block to proper mathematical notation, you would need to restore the dependence upon k. For example, the equation that would appear in the code:

```
x=y+1.0,
```

corresponds to the mathematical equation:
$$x[k] = y[k] + 1.0, \text{ for } k>0.$$
The only time the dependence upon k appears is in the definition of lagged variables.

Note. *Currently, lagged variables have to be defined as separate variables, and then used within other expressions. I use the convention of putting "LAG" in front of the original variable name to get the name of the lagged variable; that is not a requirement. In the future, the equation parser may support directly including lagged variables within expressions, eliminating the need to declare them as new variables.*

The treatment of time zero $(k=0)$ is special. We are working with a vector difference equation, and we normally need to define the entire state vector at $k=0$ for the solution to be well-defined. However, the system allows users to define the initial conditions only partially, using the following rules.

- Exogenous variables always use the first entry of the list defining the exogenous variable values.
- Initial conditions that are explicitly stated are always used.
- Endogenous variables that evaluate to constants use that constant value. (As implied by the previous step, if an initial condition is set, that overrides the constant.)
- If it is possible to evaluate the expression for a variable using known initial conditions, then that value is used.

- Otherwise, the initial condition for a particular variable is set to zero.

(Please note that it is possible to have the solver attempt to find an initial steady state; please see Section 4.5 for details.)

The fact that explicitly set initial conditions override expressions on the right-hand side of equations explains why the mathematical equivalent for the Python equations includes the condition that $k>0$.

Note that there is nothing in these rules about initial conditions to ensure that accounting identities will hold. It is up to the user to ensure that initial conditions result in balance sheets balancing. That is, if you set the initial Treasury bill assets of the household sector to be 100.0 at $k=0$, you will also need to ensure that you adjust the associated liability entry of the issuer of Treasury bills as well (either the Treasury or consolidated government). Not being careful with initial conditions is the most likely cause of accounting inconsistencies; once the model is running, much of the accounting is handled by framework-generated equations.

Within the expressions used, the user can use other variables, constants, built-in functions, or any function that is in the built-in *math* module (exp, sin, etc.). (The package imports the objects from the *math* module, so that they do not need to be preceded with "math.".) If the user wants to define a custom function, you call the AddFunction() method of the EquationSolver object.

Since the expressions are evaluated by the Python compiler, certain keywords cannot be used. For example, import and yield are reserved. The functions get_invalid_variable_names and get_invalid_tokens, defined in sfc_models.utils, list variable names and tokens (components of equations) that are rejected.

For example (partial code):

```
def f(x):
    return x*x + 2.0
my_model.EquationSolver(function_name='f', function_object=f)
```

Note that we do not have to assign the function to the same name as the original function definition (we could set function_name to g if we wanted to refer to the function that way within expressions. Also, the ability to treat the function f as an object that can be passed into the method may be surprising to users of other languages.

4.4 Solution Method

The solution method used in Version 1.0 of the *sfc_models* framework is a standard iterative solution technique. There is no guarantee that the solver will find a solution. The solution method has been adequate to find a solution for all of the models considered so far (based on those in Godley and Lavoie's *Monetary Economics*). A heuristic has been incorporated to help convergence for some trickier models.

The adequacy of the solver has meant that there was no pressure to find a better algorithm. There are presumably better algorithms already available in Python. The downside of incorporating such algorithms is that they create a dependency upon external packages, which can be difficult to install for some users. (The author did have difficulties in installing the *matplotlib* on a number of different Windows™ computers.) Since the base *sfc_models* package works with just the standard Python library, it is very easy for users to replicate the results in examples without other installations. (Such users would be missing chart plotting capabilities.)

The base algorithm is straightforward, and is a standard technique used in the proof of the *Contraction Mapping Theorem* (also known as a fixed-point theorem). For example, this algorithm is used in Section 14 of Chapter 2 of *Elements of the Theory of Functions and Functional Analysis* by A.N. Kolmogorov and S.V. Fomin.

We place all the variables for a single time period in a vector labelled x. (This means that if there are 10 variables to be solved, x is a 10 dimensional vector.) We refer to this vector as a *state vector*; it represents the current state of the system. We want to solve the equation:

$$x = f(x).$$

The solution method:

- Start with an initial guess, labelled x_0. This is the solution from the previous time period, or the initial conditions.
- Solve for a new vector x_1, with $x_1 = f(x_0)$.
- Repeat evaluating the function f, until the change in the vector between iterations (that is, the difference between x_{k+1} and x_k) is "sufficiently small," or the maximum number of iterations has been hit. In the latter case, the code throws a Conver-

`genceError` indicating a lack of convergence.

The criterion for determining whether changes in a vector are "sufficiently small" to be considered the final solution is defined so as to be insensitive to the magnitude of the variables. If we looked at the absolute value of the changes of all the variables, the convergence time would depend upon the magnitude of the variables. If variables are in the billions or trillions (matching dollar sizes of Gross Domestic Product), just rounding errors that occur would be enough to violate an error tolerance that is acceptable for variables of around 10 or 100. The criterion chosen was to sum up the "relative errors" for each variable independently. This is defined as:

- The absolute change in the variable, if that magnitude is less than 10^{-3} (denoted 1e-3 in code).
- Otherwise, the absolute change in the variable, divided by a scaling factor. The scaling factor is the maximum of the absolute values of the original or new value of the variable. (The maximum is chosen to ensure that we do not divide by zero. Since we know that the difference of the old and new values is greater than 10^{-3}, we know that either the new or old value has a magnitude of at least 10^{-3}.)

If there are problems with convergence, it is possible to set the `TraceStep` parameter of the equation solver to cause it to output the values of variables during each iteration into the 'step' log file (created by `RegisterStandardLogs`, as discussed in Section 3.3). That is, if you add:

```
modelobject.EquationSolver.TraceStep = 7
```

to your code before calling `main()`, the iteration results for the time step $k=7$ will be output to the "step" log file, which has the extension "_iteration.txt".

One thing to keep in mind when looking at this log file is that not all variables are solved at each iteration. Some variables are identified as being "decorative": no other variable depends upon them within the set of equations. It is wasteful to calculate them during each iteration; instead, they are only calculated once the algorithm has converged. The equations are parsed by an `EquationParser` object, and it may not be obvious which variables will end up being classified as decorative.

It should be noted that there is no guarantee that there are no other solutions to the equation $x = f(x)$; that is, uniqueness is not ensured. If there are an infinite number of solutions that form a connected set, it is likely that the algorithm will fail to converge (as it might jump around different points in the set of solutions). Furthermore, there is no guarantee that the algorithm will converge to a solution, even if it exists.

The question arises: for what cases will the algorithm find a solution? The *Contraction Mapping Theorem* describes a condition for which we can guarantee that a solution exists and is unique. (The rest of this paragraph lapses into mathematical jargon, and may be safely skipped.) The condition is that the vector norm of *f(x)-f(y)* is strictly less than the norm of *x-y*, for *x* not equal to *y*. (There are many possible vector norms, but a standard choice is to use the Euclidean norm – the square root of the sum of the squares of the entries of the vector.)

The *Contraction Mapping Theorem* is a conservative result, as it is possible for a unique solution to exist while the contraction mapping condition does not hold. The standard mathematical phrasing is that it is a sufficient condition, but not a necessary one. However, validating whether the condition holds would be difficult in most cases; the easiest way to test convergence is to run the algorithm and see what happens. In most cases, examination of the step trace explains what is causing the lack of convergence.

There is one *heuristic* added to this standard algorithm used to help convergence. (Heuristic is mathematical jargon; it can be viewed as a polite way of saying "educated guess.") It was needed to allow a Gold Standard model to converge. The problem is easiest to explain in the context of that Gold Standard Model, and so the discussion of the heuristic is deferred to Section 6.5, after the Gold Standard model is introduced.

4.5 Initial Steady State

One typical task in SFC modelling is examining the effect of a policy change. We assume that a model starts in a *steady state* at *k=0*, the policy change hits at some later time, and we then examine the solution. (A *steady state* is a point in the state space for which model variables stay at the same value as time passes, barring some external shock to the system. I will not attempt to give a formal definition; one is available in *Monetary Economics*. We are using the definition of state vector found in the previous section: it is a set of variable values stacked up in a column, which is referred to as a vector in linear algebra.) This yields more plausible scenarios than starting with stock variables (such as debt levels) equal to zero. However, the difficulty with this task is that we need to set the initial conditions of the variables to equal the initial steady state.

This is particularly difficult if there are multiple types of financial assets within the model. All need to be set at levels that match asset allocation functions, and we must ensure that all balance sheets balance. (At present, the framework does not attempt to force balance sheets into balance; unbalanced initial conditions result in the creation of "ghost asset balances" that are implied but not explicitly held within the model.)

The `EquationSolver` class has the capacity to solve for an initial steady state (if it exists). By setting `ParameterSolveInitial-SteadyState` to `True`, the solver will starts a new simulation, starting at *k=-200* (by default), and then simulating from that point until *k=0*. If simulation variables have converged to fixed levels, we use those levels as the initial steady state. The solver will then restart from *k=0* from that steady state value normally. (The starting time is set by `ParameterInitialSteadyStateMaxTime`, which has a default of 200.)

Importantly, if this option is chosen, the initial conditions are applied to the starting state in negative time; the values at *k=0* are just the calculated steady state values. By default, all financial stock variables start at zero, and therefore balance sheets balance. Therefore, the resulting steady state (if it exists) will obey accounting rules. (If the user hardcodes an initial condition, it is up to the user to validate that accounting consistency holds.) It is not possible to solve for a steady state and then specify different initial conditions for *k=0*. That is, you would not be able to apply a shock to the steady state until *k=1*.

It would be more elegant to solve for the steady state explicitly (as is done in the text *Monetary Economics*). In principle, it looks straightforward: we just leave the equations unchanged, except for lag conditions. In a steady state, $x[k-1] = x[k]$. That is, we replace lag relationships with an equality. However, when this solution technique was tested for simple models, the system of equations did not converge (with the existing solver). It is a future research project to re-examine this.

The framework currently only supports the notion of a constant steady state: (almost) all variables are assumed to converge to constant values. (Exceptions are discussed below.) Presumably, we need exogenous variables to be constant as well. As a result, we use the value of exogenous variables at $k=0$ for all negative times. This technique will not work for variables that are viewed as "exogenous" from the point of view of economics, but are not explicitly defined as such. For example, we might think of government consumption as exogenous, and we want to see what happens if it increases linearly. If we specify spending as a function (for example, G = 20 * k) government spending will be calculated as such during negative time. As a result, we would not expect a steady state solution to exist. However, if we define G as an exogenous variable, equal to a Python list ([0.0, 20.0, 40.0, ...]), the government spending will be held flat at 0 for all negative time. If you want to avoid using a list, you could define the variable to be equal to a custom function (Section 7.3). You just need to ensure that the custom function returns a constant value for negative time values.

In this case, we could use:

```
def gov_spending(k):
    """
    Government spending function that respects neg-
ative time.
    """
    if k < 0:
        # We are in the initial steady state calcu-
lation
        return 0.0
    else:
        return 20.0*k
```

The calculated time series are associated with the 'steadystate_0' log, which is output to the "_steadystate.txt" log when RegisterStandardLogs is called (Section 3.3). This log will need to be examined to see which series do not reach steady state in the case of a convergence error.

The framework looks at the last values to see whether they are (roughly) constant. The criterion may be changed in the future; it presently just looks at the last two values, and checks whether the percentage change is less than ParameterInitialSteadyStateErrorToler (default is now 10^{-4} or 1e-4). The exception is when the last value is small in absolute terms (this is a hardcoded threshold of 1e-4). In this case, the algorithm just validates that the previous value has a similarly low absolute value. This needs to be done, as series that are close to zero can have quite large percentage changes when solved numerically.

However, some variables are expected to change, even in a steady state. The most obvious example being the custom time axis t. The parameter `ParameterInitialSteadyStateExcludedVariables` is a parameter that is a list of variables to exclude (by default, just 't'). (The time axis k is always excluded.) The user can add more variables to exclude in order to proceed to solving in positive time.

A planned extension will be to allow a "steady state" where variables are growing at a steady rate. Unfortunately, the growth rate of variables depends upon the variables' classification. For example, nominal variables will grow at a nominal growth rate, real variables at a real growth rate, and price variables the rate of inflation. Meanwhile, parameters will still be constants, with a nominal growth rate of zero. The complexity of determining whether the solution is a legitimate steady state explains why this implementation has been pushed back.

Chapter 5 Closed Economy Models

5.1 Introduction

This chapter explains how to develop economic models where there is only a single country within the model. Such models are typically referred to as *closed economy* models, as the economy is closed to trade. When we allow for international trade, we are discussing *open economy* models, which are the subject of Chapter 6.

These models are easy to deal with as we assume that there is a single currency within the model. This makes accounting straightforward. Furthermore, with a single central government, we only have a single issuer of "money" or "Treasury bills."

In addition to a model with only a single `Country` object, we can include the special case where we have multiple countries, but no transactions between them. Although this does not appear to be useful from a pure modelling standpoint, it can be a useful programming trick. We can create a single model that includes two countries that differ in some manner, and we can then directly compare the two sets of data. Since many of the analysis support tools were designed to work with a single model, this technique may be easier to work with than setting up two separate models. For example, the variables in the two `Country` objects will be differentiated by their country codes, and it would be possible to compare variables side-by-side within the output csv file.

This chapter also offers some background on the characteristics of SFC models. The operation of some basic models taken from Godley and Lavoie's *Monetary Economics* is explained. The next section will discuss the relationship to that text in more detail.

5.2 Relationship to "Monetary Economics"

The text *Monetary Economics: An Integrated Approach to Credit, Money, Income, Production and Wealth*, by Wynne Godley and Marc Lavoie is cited heavily within this book, and within the *sfc_models* framework. This text is a standard text for SFC modelling, and has already been the object of extensive computer implementation. The fact that the models are well known is extremely useful from the point of view of development. These existing implementations were used to calibrate the *sfc_models* code.

Users who wish to implement the models directly from *Monetary Economics* can do so by using the code in the `sfc_models.gl_book` sub-package. There are modules within the `gl_book` package that correspond to the chapters of the book. (In some cases, there are multiple models within each chapter.) At the time of writing, the coverage of models is quite selective, but more may be added over time. It is possible to build the models quickly by loading them from the `sfc_models.gl_book` sub-package, or it is possible to examine the source code for the chapter modules to see the operations to create the models directly. The method to load the models directly from the library is given below. However, if you wish to experiment with the models, it would be best to build them by copying the source code into new files. The code in the `gl_book` sub-package is designed to emulate the models in the book exactly, as this is needed for calibration.

This calibration effort may be invisible to most users of the *sfc_models* package, but it is a key reason why the package should be a stable programming environment. As discussed in Section 2.5, Python has well-developed unit testing capabilities. Other than some areas of code that inherently cannot be tested – and are explicitly marked as such – the objective is that 100% of the lines of code be exercised in tests. These unit tests call functions and methods, and ensure that the output matches expectations.

Code that is designed to be unit tested needs to be broken into small blocks; spaghetti code has to be avoided. Each of the small components is tested separately, so that desired changes to one block do not break hundreds of tests (forcing the tests to be re-written, or abandoned).

The risk with testing of this nature is that we are focused on testing small parts, and it may be possible that changes will cause errors in unexpected ways due to unforeseen interactions. Therefore, we need to augment smaller unit tests with *end-to-end tests*. These end-to-end tests launch large operations, but only examine the final results; intermediate implementation details are allowed to remain flexible. For *sfc_models*, the model outputs from selected models from *Monetary Economics* were used as end-to-end tests. Since the models were implemented elsewhere already, the target output data (based on fixed inputs) were already available. It was possible to use these target data to ensure that the models generated by *sfc_models* matched the existing results.

It would have been possible to have *sfc_models* generate models that behaved differently than those in *Monetary Economics*. However, such models would be non-standard, and one of the first things users may want to do is emulate the models in *Monetary Economics*. Rather than start from an unorthodox position (an *unorthodox heterodox position?*), I instead decided to be able to emulate the existing structures in *Monetary Economics* perfectly, and leave the job of creating new types of models as future extensions under the control of users.

One difference between the *sfc_models* framework and that of Godley and Lavoie is the equation structure. Since the *sfc_models* equations are generated algorithmically, they needed to be set up in a generic fashion that allows the algorithms to create connections between sectors in a flexible manner. As a result, the initial set of equations generated by *sfc_models* features many redundant equations (that are pruned by the solver). This destroys some of the mathematical elegance. A second difference is cosmetic: variables in `sfc_models` are based on an algorithmic scheme based on long text strings, while Godley and Lavoie use standard variable names from economics, using mathematical notation with subscripts. Therefore, the user needs to "translate" variable names when comparing results. The final difference is a limitation of the `sfc_models` framework: there is no mechanism to generate the transaction matrices that are a prominent feature of *Monetary Economics*. It may be possible to infer such matrices from the economic model structure, but the feasibility of that step has not yet been examined.

To create the models directly from gl_book, the user needs to invoke model builder objects. They create a `Model` object, and optionally set the exogenous variables to match the book output. The model builder objects are defined in the modules in gl_book, which are named after the associated chapter in *Monetary Economics*. For example, to create the model REG from Chapter 6, the following syntax is used.

```
import sfc_models
from sfc_models.gl_book.chapter6 import REG
```

```
builder_REG = REG(country_code='C1', use_book_
exogenous=True)
model = builder_REG.build_model()
```

The model object returned by `build_model` is a Model object that can be worked with in the same manner as one created manually. Setting the *use_book_exogenous* parameter to *True* causes the framework to use the same values of exogenous variables as were used in the examples in *Monetary Economics*. By setting it to *False*, you can experiment with different inputs.

The rest of this chapter discusses some basic models that are (mainly) taken from *Monetary Economics*. The discussion offers some economic insight into them, but not at the level of depth seen in that text. Instead, the objective is to give an informal explanation of the operations of these models.

5.3 Intuitive Model Solution

This section describes the solution of the simplest non-trivial SFC model – labelled "model SIM" in Godley and Lavoie's *Monetary Economics* (Chapter 3). The simplicity of this model is a great advantage. It is possible to describe various properties of SFC models using a model whose properties can be understood without requiring much mathematics. Its scope is of course limited; it could not be used to predict business cycles.

In this section, I am describing how the model solution is derived for a single period using intuitive (yet correct) mathematical and accounting arguments. Under normal circumstances, we rely on setting up the equations defining the model and solving them (or let *sfc_models* do that work). However, unless the reader wants to dig through the algebra, this can leave the intuition behind what the solution represents underdeveloped. We need to have this intuition in order to understand the properties of these models; as otherwise, the output becomes a black box. For casual users of *sfc_models*, this lack of intuition may not matter, but it poses a risk for anyone doing research that is more advanced. If we do not know what to expect, we could easily make a mistake when configuring a new model, and not even realise the problem.

In order to be able to solve the model without referring to the full set of equations, the model is stripped down to be even simpler than the version found in Godley and Lavoie. We are starting at time zero *(t=0)* with no pre-existing financial asset stocks, and the tax rate is equal to zero. (The latter assumption leads to a pathological model, but it simplifies the solution technique for the first period.)

The simulation starts at $t=0$. (As a technical aside, *sfc_models* normally uses k as the discrete time variable that denotes the time step that always starts at $k=0$, while t is "real world time", like January 2000. This convention is based upon the conventions of electrical engineering, where there can be a mixture of discrete time and continuous time axes in analysis. This section uses t instead of k since that convention is probably more familiar.) We assume that there is very little happening before then, or $t<0$. There is no government money, and no economic activity, although we somehow have a labour force and capital in place at $t=0$. This is obviously unrealistic, but to be expected in a mathematical model.

The government starts issuing money at $t=1$. It kicks off economic activity by ordering $20 worth of services (produced by the business sector, as described below.) As noted earlier, we assume that government taxation is zero during the first period. This is different from the configuration in *Monetary Economics*, which means that the results derived here do not match the numbers given there (or the standard SIM model in `sfc_models.gl_book.chapter3`).

Since we are fixing government spending to be $20 for this period, and taxes are zero, we know that the government sector must run a fiscal deficit of $20 in the period. The only financial asset within this economy is government money, and so we know that the private sector will hold $20 in money at the end of the period. (Normally in model SIM, the amount of taxes levied depends upon economic activity. By eliminating taxation, solving the equations is much simpler.)

For simplicity, we assume that there is an unlimited number of workers available within the household sector. As a result, there is no concept of an "unemployment rate"; there are a number of employed workers and an infinite pool of unemployed workers. This is the standard behaviour of the `Household` sector object; a proper modelling of the unemployment rate is a future extension.

The household sector works for the business sector, receiving wages. (Normally, it would also pay taxes based on wages received.) Not all wages are spent; some are saved and the household ends the period holding money. How much is saved is discussed below.

The business sector is assumed to hold capital (that does not depreciate) with infinite productive capacity; output is solely dependent upon labour inputs. Production is linear: for every worker hired, there will be an output of one unit of services. Services cannot be held in inventory, so there is no need to track the stock (level) of inventories.

All prices are administered. This is done in a simple fashion to allow the model to remain linear. The business firm has taken the notion of "non-profit" to an extreme: it pays each worker $1 over the period, and charges $1 for one unit of output. (Since the worker produces 1 unit, the firm has zero profit on every unit sold, assuming all units are sold.)

The cash flows during the first period are illustrated below.

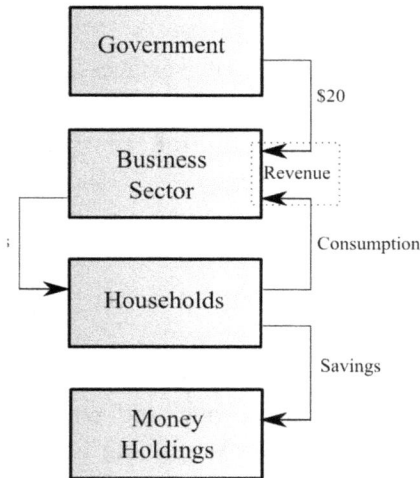

Another simplification of model SIM is that the only financial asset holdings within the economy are by the household sector. This means that the business sector cannot hold money at the end of the period, and has no profits. As a result, the total business sector revenue (which equals government spending of $20 plus household consumption) has to equal the wage bill by assumption.

This implies a form of "model-consistent expectations." The business sector somehow has to forecast its total revenue accurately in order to determine the number of workers hired. If it did not, it could potentially incur a loss, which is assumed not to occur.

Model-consistent expectations represent a subset of rational expectations. Rational expectations are heavily criticised by post-Keynesian academics as being unrealistic; model-consistent expectations can be hit with the same critiques. The assumption can be relaxed, at the cost of making the model more complex. We would need to add a function that gives an estimate of business revenue, and the business sector would hire based on that estimated level of demand. The error between forecast and realised revenue would generate new model dynamics.

Since we assume that wage expense equals business sector revenue, we can inspect the diagram to see that the solution implies that the household sector saves $20. Beyond that, the model is still under-determined. That is, if our only constraint is that accounting relationships hold (plus our added assumptions about profits), there are an infinite number of solutions.

- The business sector could hire 20 workers to produce the services demanded by the government, and those workers could save 100% of their wages. Total business revenue is $20.
- The business sector could hire 1000 workers, and those workers spend most of their wages ($980 out of $1000). Total business revenue is $1000.

This is unrealistic. Part of the lack of realism reflects the assumption about an infinite labour supply. Nevertheless, even if we modelled capital and labour constraints, there would be a range of potential solutions. In other words, accounting relationships are not enough. We need to add a description of entity behaviour within the model.

The model needs a mechanism to pin down how much the household sector spends versus saves. (Looking at the previous diagram, we see that the household use of money is the only decision point within the model: all other flows are determined.) Stock-Flow Consistent models opt for straightforward consumption functions. The standard form used in *sfc_ models* is:

```
DEM_GOODS = AlphaIncome * AfterTax + AlphaFin *
LAG_F,
```

(assuming that we use the standard label "GOODS" for the consumption good). This code fragment is found in the `BaseHousehold` class, found in `sfc_models.sector_definitions`. The parameters

`AlphaIncome` and `AlphaFin` are the propensity to consume of after-tax income (`AfterTax`) or the previous period's net financial wealth
(`LAG_F`). Note that the first parameter relates a flow to a flow, and would
be invariant to the time scale. The second relates a stock variable (wealth)
to a flow variable (spending), and so would need to be adjusted if the time
scale changes. For example, if a household spends an amount that is 1%
of its wealth in a month, it would roughly translate into 12% per year.

For period *t=1* in my simplified model, initial money holdings are 0,
and so the consumption function is simplified by dropping the second
term. Moreover, since taxes are assumed to be zero, the after-tax income equals pre-tax income, which is equal to the aggregate wage bill.

For example, if `AlphaIncome`=*0.6*, we can back out that the aggregate wage bill has to be $50, since the household savings of $20 is 40% of
$50. (Full formula: *Total Wages = $20/(1-AlphaIncome).*) A lower personal
savings rate (higher `AlphaIncome`) implies a greater level of wages and
output. Total output (GDP) equals government and household consumption. This means that GDP is $50 in the period, since business sector
output equals the wage bill.

A great deal of analysis refers to *multipliers* on government spending. In
this case, $20 in government spending generates $50 in GDP (or a multiplier of 2.5). Given the linearity of the relationships within this model,
GDP will scale up if government spending is scaled up. That is, $40 in
spending in period 0 will result in GDP of $100.

However, the multiplier above is for one period. If we keep the amount
of spending constant, GDP will continue to increase until it reaches a
"steady state" level. In other words, the long-run multiplier is larger than
the short-run multiplier. This is seen in the simulation results previously
presented in Section 3.2.

The multiplier process is somewhat unsettling from the perspective of
translation to the real world. Imagine that the model frequency is daily. The
business sector was previously mired in a state of no activity whatsoever.
It suddenly receives a government contract for $20. Certainly, the recipi-
ent of the contract would quickly hire at least 20 workers (at $1 each) to
be able to fulfil the contract. (Remember that the business sector always
breaks even.) However, would it hire an additional 30 workers that same
day, on the basis of the expected circular flows of revenue within the

economy? Moreover, in the real world, there are multiple firms, and revenue would be split up amongst them. Until revenue starts to come in, why would they start hiring?

This implausibility suggests that we should replace "perfect foresight" expectations with a version of expectations that allows for errors. In this case, the multiplier effect would work with more of a lag. This would be particularly true if demand is met from inventories; firms can wait for inventories to be unusually depleted (relative to sales) before ramping up production.

Conversely, if the time period within the model is annual, businesses would notice increased activity during the year. One would expect hiring and output to ramp up within the model time step, and reach a steady state before the end of the accounting period. In such a case, model-consistent expectations may be a good approximation of reality.

These considerations mean that we cannot expect model dynamics to be similar across different model frequencies. That said, the difficulties faced by fitting these models to data are so large that this is hardly our greatest worry.

We can validate the analysis above by building the model using *sfc_models*.

File: intro_5_03_no_tax_SIM.py

```
# This next line imports all of the objects used.
# The syntax "from <module> import *" is frowned
upon, but I want to reduce the number of lines of
# code in these simpler examples.
from sfc_models.objects import *
from sfc_models.examples.Quick2DPlot import Quick-
2DPlot


# The next line of code sets the name of the output
files based on the code file's name.
# This means that if you paste this code into a new
file, get a new log name.
register_standard_logs('output', __file__)
# Create model, which holds all entities
mod = Model()
# Create first country - Canada. (This model only
has one country.)
can = Country(mod, 'CA', 'Canada')
```

```
# Create sectors
gov = ConsolidatedGovernment(can, 'GOV',
 'Government')
hh = Household(can, 'HH', 'Household')
# A literally non-profit business sector
bus = FixedMarginBusiness(can, 'BUS', 'Business
Sector')
labour = Market(can, 'LAB', 'Labour market')
goods = Market(can, 'GOOD', 'Goods market')
# Need to set the exogenous variable - Government
demand for Goods ("G" in economist symbology)
mod.AddExogenous('GOV', 'DEM_GOOD', '[20.,] * 105')
# Build the model
mod.main()
CUT = 10
k = mod.GetTimeSeries('k', cutoff=CUT)
goods_produced = mod.GetTimeSeries('BUS__SUP_GOOD',
cutoff=CUT)
print('Goods Production at time 1 = {0}'.
format(goods_produced[1]))
Quick2DPlot(k, goods_produced, 'Goods Produced (Na-
tional Output)')
```

If run, the `print` statement shows us that the output at *t=1* is equal to 50 (within rounding errors).

If we compare to the model specification of Model SIM (found in `sfc_models.gl_book.chapter3.py`), we see that there is one line missing:

```
tax = TaxFlow(country, 'TF', 'TaxFlow', taxrate=.2)
```

This is the line that creates a `TaxFlow Sector` object that sets up the taxation flows in the country, with a tax rate of 20%. If the output of the above model is examined, it can be seen that output is steadily increasing and is not reaching a limiting value. This tells us that there is no steady state solution for the model.

5.4 Expectations

Household expectations appear in Model SIMEX, described in Chapter 3 of Godley and Lavoie's *Monetary Economics*. The name reflects the fact that this is Model SIM (the simplest SFC model), augmented with the effect of expectations upon household consumption.

The consumption function used within model SIMEX is (using the *sfc_models* variable name convention):

```
DEM_GOOD = AlphaIncome * EXP_AfterTax + AlphaFin *
LAG_F,
```

where:

- DEM_GOOD = demand for goods (i.e., consumption),
- EXP_AfterTax is the expected after-tax income,
- LAG_F = the previous period's financial asset holdings (denoted F within sfc_models),
- and AlphaIncome, AlphaFin are the propensity to consume of income and wealth, respectively.

This is an "old Keynesian" consumption function, where it is driven by the current level of income and financial asset holdings.

By comparison, within Model SIM, the equation is:

```
DEM_GOOD = AlphaIncome * AfterTax + AlphaFin *
LAG_F.
```

That is, the only difference is that Model SIM uses actual (realised) after-tax income, rather than expected income. Since after-tax income is determined by the simultaneous solution of all of the model equations within the period, Model SIM implies that the household has the ability to calculate exactly the current period model solution (and hence income). This is referred to as "perfect foresight," although it does not technically imply an ability to predict *future* outcomes.

Monetary Economics discusses two differing ways in which the expectations variable is determined. I will now discuss the first variant, which is labelled "SIMEX1" within the *sfc_models* package. In SIMEX1, the expected after-tax income is the previous period's realised after-tax income, or

```
EXP_AfterTax(k) = AfterTax(k-1).
```

(Within the earlier equations, the dependence upon the time axis ("*k*") is suppressed, following the equation convention used within the Python package. As discussed below, this equation is only used for $k>1$, $k=0$ and $k=1$ are special cases.)

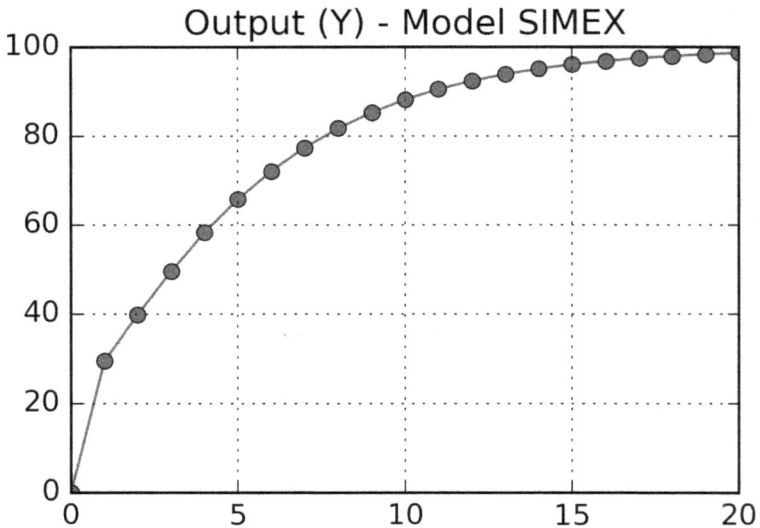

Output (Y) - Model SIMEX

We will now look at an example of economic trajectory (shown above). The model starts in a state of zero activity, and then the government generates activity by starting a programme of constant government purchases ("*G*") of $20 per period. The private sector responds, and aggregate output ("*Y*") converges towards the steady state value of $100. (This means that the multiplier on *G* is 5; the simplicity of the model implies that government spending alone determines the steady state output level.)

We can now examine the expected household after-tax income variable (next figure).

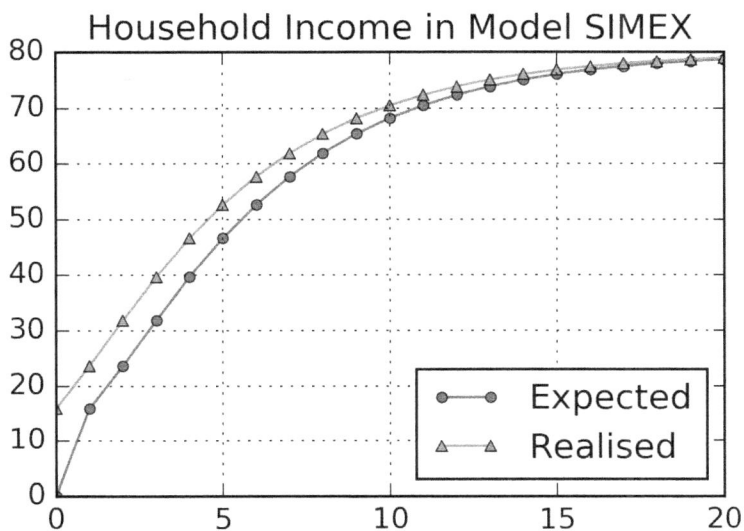

Household Income in Model SIMEX

As can be seen in the chart, the expected income is just the previous period's income. At first, there is a large difference (forecast error), but the error decreases as the income converges towards its steady state value. (Please note that behaviour at the first time period – $k=0$ – is somewhat unusual; this is discussed later)

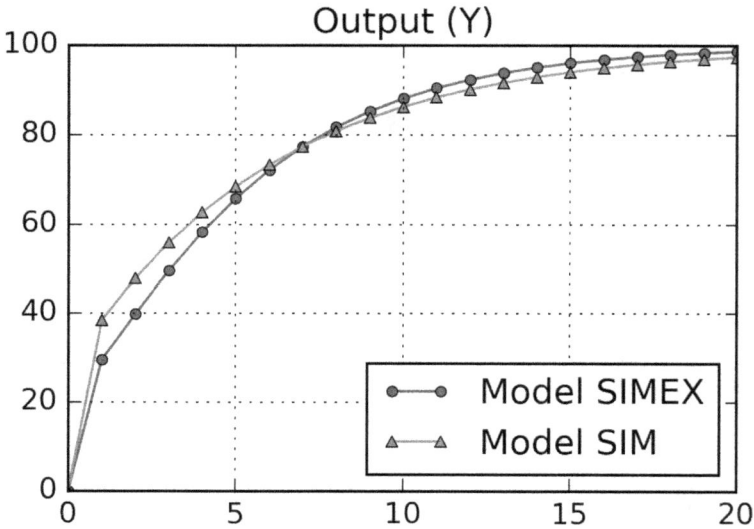

The figure above shows the effect of using expected income rather than actual income in a model. We look at model SIM and SIMEX with the same behavioural parameters, and apply the same exogenous (external) input (government spending). In the earlier periods, the household sector reacts more quickly to the rise in income, and so aggregate output rises more quickly. As one might expect, the use of more accurate expectations results in a quicker response to policy changes. It should be noted that both models converge to the same steady state value. The reason why there is a crossover of the two time series around time period 7 is explained further below.

The counterpart to the miss in income expectations in spending is that the household sector's financial asset holdings evolve in a different fashion. Financial assets act as a cushion for errors in forecasting income and expenditures, a point that is emphasised in post-Keynesian writings.

The next figure shows the evolution of financial asset holdings by the household sector. Since the household sector is consistently under-estimating its income in Model SIMEX, it consumes less than in model SIM in the early time periods. As a result, it ends up with greater financial asset holdings. Since spending also depends upon the stock of financial asset holdings, the consumption flow that is related to wealth is larger in SIMEX. By time period 8, this larger consumption flow out of assets means that output in SIMEX ends up being higher than in SIM. This is why the plotted output levels (Y) cross over in the chart.

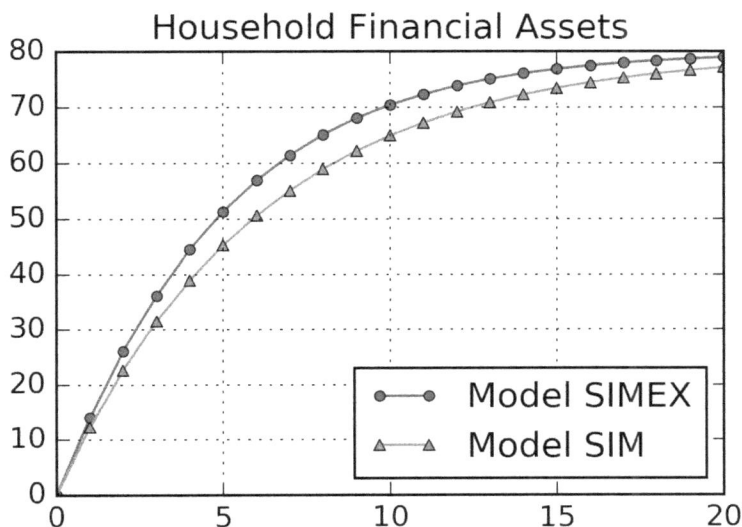

Household Financial Assets

The role of financial assets is to act as a stabiliser within the model. Even with missed income expectations, output ends up roughly where it would have been otherwise, as the lower spending out of income (due to too-low expectations) is compensated by greater spending out of financial asset holdings. The importance of such stock variables is the reason why these models are referred to as stock-flow consistent models; flow behaviour is consistent with the behaviour of stocks. In other words, the name does not just imply that the accounting is done correctly (which is a common interpretation).

Additionally, the fact that stock variables acted to compensate for incorrect expectations about flows implies that expectations are not extremely important for model outcomes. This is very different from modern mainstream economics, which revolves around the role of expectations.

There is a final technical point regarding the simulation results shown above. Model SIMEX in section 3.7.2 of *Monetary Economics* starts with a special case for expected income. In period 1 of the book's simulations, the expected household income is not equal to the previous period's income (which was $0), rather it took into account the surge in government spending G. For period 1, the household assumes that total output is equal to G, and so its pre-tax income is equal to $20 (and the after-tax income is $16). It is only in later periods that the expected income is equal to the realised after-tax income.

This special case is simulated within Python code by forcing the realised after-tax income variable (HH_AfterTax) to be $16 at $k=0$. This is why the after-tax income is non-zero in the first period in the figure above. (I misinterpreted the explanation for this special case when I read *Monetary Economics*; I would like to thank Marc Lavoie for patiently pointing out the passage that explains the special case.)

This workaround creates an inconsistency at $k=0$, but that is not viewed as problematic within the *sfc_models* framework: there is no attempt to solve the system of equations at $k=0$, and so it is sometimes preferable to drop that point from system output.

File intro_5_04_SIMEX1.py

```
import os
import sfc_models
from sfc_models.gl_book.chapter3 import SIMEX1, SIM
from sfc_models.examples.Quick2DPlot import Quick-
2DPlot

# The next line of code sets the name of the output
files based on the code file's name.
# This means that if you paste this code into a new
file, get a new log name.
sfc_models.register_standard_logs('output',
__file__)
builder_SIMEX = SIMEX1(country_code='C1',
use_book_exogenous=True)
model = builder_SIMEX.build_model()

model.main()

# NOTE: Running two models messes up file output...
builder_SIM = SIM(country_code='C1', use_book_
exogenous=True)
```

```
model_SIM = builder_SIM.build_model()
model_SIM.main()

model.TimeSeriesCutoff = 20
model_SIM.TimeSeriesCutoff = 20
time = model.GetTimeSeries('k')
Y_SIMEX = model.GetTimeSeries('GOOD__SUP_GOOD')
Y_SIM = model_SIM.GetTimeSeries('GOOD__SUP_GOOD')
income = model.GetTimeSeries('HH__AfterTax')
expected_income = model.GetTimeSeries('HH__EXP_Af-
terTax')
F_SIMEX = model.GetTimeSeries('HH__F')
F_SIM = model_SIM.GetTimeSeries('HH__F')
Quick2DPlot(time, Y_SIMEX, 'Output (Y) - Model
SIMEX')
q = Quick2DPlot([time, time], [expected_income, in-
come], 'Household Income in Model SIMEX',
run_now=False, filename='SIMEX1_output.png')
q.Legend = ['Expected', 'Realised']
q.DoPlot()
q = Quick2DPlot([time, time], [Y_SIMEX, Y_SIM],
'Output (Y)', run_now=False)
q.Legend = ['Model SIMEX', 'Model SIM']
q.DoPlot()
q = Quick2DPlot([time, time], [F_SIMEX, F_SIM],
'Household Financial Assets', run_now=False)
q.Legend = ['Model SIMEX', 'Model SIM']
q.DoPlot()
```

As can be seen in the code, the meat of the model description is embedded within model builder objects that are found in the `sfc_mod-els.gl_book.chapter3` module. This is a feature that allows the user to quickly reconstruct the models within *Monetary Economics*.

5.5 Central Banks

Central banks are often a feature of economic models. The role of the central bank is to supply money, which pays no interest, while the Treasury (fiscal arm of the central government) supplies interest-bearing instruments (typically Treasury bills).

The importance of central banks in the context of many macro models is debatable. For models that resemble most floating-currency sovereign states – such as the United States, Japan, or Canada – this level of detail is largely irrelevant to the model outcome. Private sector money and Treasury bill holdings are determined by the policy rate of interest, and the central bank operations are forced to conform to the desired portfolio holdings. We could consolidate (merge) the central bank with the Treasury, and the model outcomes will essentially be the same. That said, the split between the central bank and Treasury matters if we have models where default by the Treasury is possible, and/or situations analogous to the euro area, where the central bank is not under control of the government. Furthermore, such a split may be needed to model the transaction patterns when the currency is pegged to an external unit – such as a foreign currency, or gold. (Such peg policies are discussed in Chapter 6.)

Central banks appear in the second group of models in Godley and Lavoie's *Monetary Economics*, in Chapter 4. The model that is implemented in *sfc_models* is referred to as Model PC (Portfolio Choice).

Within the model, there are two financial assets: money and government bills. (Readers familiar with my other writings will note that I did not follow my own advice from the book *Abolish Money (From Economics)!* – since money indeed appears within the framework. It should be noted that the role of "money" in the framework does correspond to how I suggest it should appear – it is just another financial asset. In any event, coming up with another label for "money" would appear quite eccentric for most users of the package.)

- The central bank is the monopoly supplier of money, which does not pay interest. (If "money" includes reserves held at the central bank, it would be necessary to create a new financial asset that pays interest.) Money is held within the private sector. (In this model, the business sector is assumed to have zero financial asset holdings, so this is just the household sector.) The amount of money outstanding is the *monetary base*.

- The Treasury is the monopoly supplier of Treasury bills, which pay interest. Treasury bills are held by the central bank and the private sector (household sector). (Within the framework, the asset name used is "deposit," since the model is using a deposit interest convention. For our purposes here, this is only a superficial detail. However, this section refers to "Treasury bills" since they are more common, and discussions of central bank buying and selling Treasury bills makes more sense than would buying or selling deposits.)

The only operations the central bank undertakes in Model PC are:

- to buy and sell Treasury bills;
- and to pay a dividend to the Treasury.

Since the liabilities of the central bank only consist of money, which pays no interest, it generates a profit based on the interest received on its Treasury bill holdings. These profits are used to pay the dividend to the Treasury.

Money creation and destruction is a concept that causes considerable confusion. We have to keep in mind that "money" in this context is just a liability of the central (which is also the case in modern economies). When the central bank buys something (in this model, treasury bills), it issues new money in exchange for whatever it buys, and so the operation creates money. Conversely, if the central bank sells a treasury bill, it transfers the treasury bill to its private sector counterparty, and the monetary liability returns to the central bank. Since the central bank does not hold its own liabilities, the liability is destroyed (and the money supply is reduced). This is exactly analogous to private sector firms issuing and redeeming debt instruments.

This structure follows the pattern of the other markets in *sfc_models*. The simplest situation for a `Market` object is that there is a monopoly of supply (a single supplier). This allows for a demand-led solution of the system of equations: supply is simply assumed to meet demand. (The more complex case is when there are multiple suppliers of the commodity traded in the market; in this case, we need to allocate demand between the suppliers.)

There is an embedded assumption that the supplier can always meet the level of demand. This is unrealistic for the product markets (goods and labour); the modelling framework needs to incorporate the supply constraints that appear in the more advanced SFC models. However, for financial assets, there are no limitations on supply: the central bank can issue as much money as it wishes in order to keep interest rates near target.

Within the model, the solution is calculated one time period at a time.

Even if we allow for expectations within the model, the model entities need to have well-defined supply and demand functions at a given time point, which allows us to calculate the solution. Therefore, even if we believe that the central bank needs to have a reaction function that determines the future path of interest rates (or the size of the monetary base), we still need to pin down its value in the current time point.

The question then arises: does the central bank set the level of interest rates, or the size of the monetary base? Within the context of Model PC, either stance is legitimate. There is a well-defined portfolio allocation function that determines the weighting of money within the household's portfolio; if we fix the interest rate, that weighting is fixed (and vice-versa). The only technical issue is the following. Since the level of household financial assets is partly determined by the current period's income, the calculation relating the *absolute* size of the monetary base and the interest rate is relatively complex. However, under normal circumstances it would be a one-to-one (invertible) function.

This would suggest that the money supply is exogenous – it can be set by the central bank. Whether the money supply is indeed exogenous is an old debate in economics; the post-Keynesian position is that it is not. However, those arguments relate to models that are more complex (or the real world); model PC is so simple that money can be viewed as exogenous. As such, the exogenous money debate cannot be resolved by this model. The convention within *Monetary Economics* is to treat the interest rate as exogenous (presumably fixed by the central bank). There is no easy to way to force the money supply to be an exogenous variable within the *sfc_models* framework; the only way in which it could be attempted is to set a target money balance as an exogenous variable, then vary the interest rate until that target balance is achieved (presuming that this is possible). This situation is realistic; even when central banks followed the fad of trying to target the growth of the money supply, they relied on an estimated demand-for-money function to choose a level of interest rates to hit the target.

Another convention used in *Monetary Economics* is for the Treasury to issue interest-bearing deposits, rather than Treasury bills issued at a discount. The deposit convention is easier to work with, but it has one side effect: the price of a deposit is par, and so we cannot engage in thought ex-

ercises regarding what would happen if the price of treasury bills instanta-
neously changed within a model time period. (Given the general confusion
such thought experiments appear to cause, this appears to be an advantage
of the present modelling convention.)

Since the money and deposit weightings are fixed once the interest rate
is set, the central bank has no discretion over how it transacts. The only degree of freedom the central bank as within the model is the management
of its equity position – how much of its profits does it pay to the Treasury
as dividends? Once the dividend policy is set, that freedom of action dis-
appears. If we take the realistic possibility that the central bank pays all of
its profits to the Treasury every period (which is the default assumption
within *sfc_models*), the central bank balance sheet is determined entirely by
private sector money demand. We can replace the `Treasury` and `Cen-
tralBank` objects with a single `ConsolidatedGovernment` ob-
ject, and no observable model data are changed in the non-governmental
sector.

The discussion of model PC continues in the next section, where the
implementation of portfolio weighting is discussed.

5.6 Portfolio Weighting

Financial assets (including "money") are an important part of stock-flow-
consistent models. There can be many types of financial assets in these
models: money, government debt, private debt, bank deposits, and equity.
The need for accounting relationships to hold (balance sheets have to balance, and inflows have to match outflows) generates considerable complexity in the model equations. The advantage of the *sfc_models* framework
is that the accounting is (largely) handled for the user.

(The exception to keep in mind is the specification of initial conditions.
It is up to the user to ensure that the initial conditions respect accounting
rules. The framework could ensure accounting consistency by forcing the
user to use high-level function(s) to specify the initial holdings. At present,
there did not appear to be a need for those high-level functions.)

The process used in *sfc_models* is straightforward. It has to be, since the
equations are being generated algorithmically. The process appears different from other treatments of financial assets in the SFC modelling literature. However, the standard technique is to generate the equations by

hand, and it is easier to create a more complex equation structure given that increased level of control. The hope is that the results of the existing models can be replicated, albeit with a superficially different set of equations.

The complexity of financial assets with models is the result of the fact that the relationships can be arrived at in multiple ways. The following statements will all be true in a well-posed economic model; however, they included redundant information. That is, it is possible to select some of the statements below that characterise financial asset holdings and flows, and use them to derive the rest.

- The change in the total value of financial asset holdings is determined by net cash flow. The net cash flow is usually equal to total income (that is, including the effect of capital gains), but we may need to add flows that do not affect income. (For example, consumption spending by the household sector does not subtract from household income.) Income is driven by flows in the real economy (wage income, goods purchases) and transfers (dividends, taxes).
- The total value of financial assets held is equal to the sum of the values of the holdings of particular instruments.
- Instruments are issued by particular sectors (for example, the Treasury/central government issues Treasury bills), and this issuance is used to finance purchases of goods or other financial assets.
- The supply of any asset has to equal its demand.

The method used to generate financial asset holdings within *sfc_models* is given by:

- The new level of a sector's financial asset holdings is equal to the previous period's financial asset holdings plus the sum of the period's cash flow terms. (At present, there are no capital gains to model. However, deposits generate interest that enters as a cash-flow term.)
- The level of holdings of any particular financial instrument for a period is equal to a weighting term times the total financial asset holding. For example, in a model where the only financial assets are money (with a 0% rate of interest) and deposits

(which pay the policy rate), the household and business sectors will allocate their portfolios between money and bills based on the rate of interest. The sum of the weightings has to be one (or else there will effectively be a ghost instrument created that catches the missing wealth).

- The supply of any financial asset is assumed to be equal to the sum of the holdings in all sectors.

The first step is the most complex, and it might be unclear what the cash flow terms refer to. Some simple examples would include:

- For a household sector that just receives wages, pays taxes, receives interest on government-issued deposits, and buys goods – household consumption. The equation is: *(new financial assets) = (old financial assets) + (wages) - (taxes) - (consumption) + (interest)*.

- A government that purchases goods and imposes taxes, and pays interest on Treasury bills: *(new financial assets) = (old financial assets) + (taxes) - (government consumption) - (interest cost)*. Since financial assets in these models are typically only government liabilities, the usual outcome is that the net financial asset holdings for the government are typically negative.

- For a business sector (in which we ignore business taxation and investment), *(new financial assets) = (old financial assets) + (total goods sales) - (wages) - (dividends)*.

These examples illustrate that these equations are mainly driven by the nominal cash flows within the real economy, such as the total wage bill, goods consumption, taxes, and interest. They do not examine how sectors "raise cash," such as the split between debt and currency issuance by the government.

It should be noted that the equations generated by the technique are solved simultaneously, and so the steps above do not tell us about the behaviour of the solution. For example, we could have the household sector's consumption depending upon money holdings, and so the "real economy" variables are not determined before the portfolio allocation step. (However, the risk is that such an information loop might cause a lack of convergence of the system of equations.)

The description taken within the framework is demand driven; the supplier of a financial instrument has no choice but to supply the amount demanded.

For example, there is no attempt to impose the governmental budget constraint (in which spending is "financed" by taxes, or the issuance of bills or money). We can back out the constraint from the system of equations, but it is purely the result of the accounting adding up properly. The total change in the government's financial position is driven by a broad fiscal deficit (with adjustments needed for the monetisation of assets, etc.), and the levels of particular liabilities (money, debt) are driven entirely by private sector portfolio allocation. (I am including the external sector under the "private sector," which might be awkward when thinking about real world data.)

Although having the supply of financial assets being driven entirely by the demand for holdings is reasonable for government liabilities, it may feel unusual for financial assets issued by the private sector. It would imply that private sector credit creation is driven entirely by credit rationing amongst the holders of financial assets, which does seem like a reasonable modelling assumption. However, under this assumption, it is nearly impossible to capture unusual positive feedback loops where a sector lends to itself. This is a relatively common occurrence in the real world, such as the household sector lending to itself as part of real estate transactions.

Asset weighting is implemented in the `GenerateAssetWeighting` method of the `Sector` class (found in *sfc_models.sector*).

This method is called to set up the weightings of financial assets for the sector. The assumption is that asset weightings are relative to the total value of financial assets, and the sum of weights equals one. (Asset weightings are specified in terms of market value of holdings.) It only needs to be called if the sector holds financial assets other than money (financial asset code default "MON"); the default behaviour is that the sector holds 100% of financial assets in the form of money.

In order to simplify the operation, if there are N financial assets, the user specifies the weighting for $N-1$. The residual asset has a weighting that is equal to 1 minus the sum of the other weights. There is no assumption that weightings are positive.

The method `Sector.GenerateAssetWeighting` has the parameters:

```
def GenerateAssetWeighting(self, asset_weighting_
dict, residual_asset_code)
```

- The parameter `asset_weight_dict` is a Python `dict` (dictionary) object that consists of a number of key/value pairs of the format: (financial asset code)/(right-hand side of weighting equation). The code for a financial asset is the short code associated with the associated `FinancialAssetMarket` object.
- The parameter *residual_asset_code* is the code for the residual asset (a string).

For example, if you want to specify that financial assets are split 50-50 between money (code= "MON") and deposits (code = "DEP"), we could call the `GenerateAssetWeighting` as follows:

```
# Needed for Python 2.7
from __future__ import print_function
# imports
from sfc_models.models import Model, Country
from sfc_models.sector import Sector
# Work
mod = Model()
can = Country(mod, 'CA')
sector_obj = Sector(can, 'SEC')
weighting_dict = {'DEP': '0.5'}
sector_obj.GenerateAssetWeighting(weighting_dict,
'MON')
print(sector_obj.Dump())
```

The output generated by the print call for the current version of *sfc_models* is:

```
[SEC] Sector Object SEC in Country CA. FullCode =
''
------------------------------------------------
DEM_DEP=F*WGT_DEP # Demand for asset DEP
DEM_MON=F*WGT_MON # Demand for asset MON
F=LAG_F # Financial assets
```

```
INC=0.0 # Income (PreTax)
LAG_F=F(k-1) # Previous periods financial assets.
WGT_DEP=0.5 # Asset weight for DEP
WGT_MON=1.0-WGT_DEP # Asset weight for MON
```

The method generated four new equations, for the terms *DEM_DEP, DEM_MON, WGT_DEP, WGT_MON*. Like other demand variables, the demand is given as a dollar amount, which is the financial asset holding ("F") times the associated weight. The weight for deposits is equal to 0.5 (as passed in), and the weight for money is equal to the residual of the other weights.

It would be possible for the user to create the demand for assets within a single equation for each asset (folding the weight variables into the demand functions), but the algebra would be more complex. The current implementation generates two added variables, but the resulting system of equations is much easier to understand and debug.

Chapter 6 Open Economy Models

6.1 Introduction

Open economy economic models are models that have more than a single country included in them. (A closed economy model is a model in which only a single country appears.) They are more complex, as we now need to represent the involved countries, as well as the interactions between them. As a result, the number of equations required for a two-country model are normally more than double that of a corresponding single economy model.

(We could reduce the complexity if we assume that a country is very small versus the rest of the world, and so the rest of the world can largely be abstracted out of existence. Such a simplification is not within the spirit of the stock-flow consistent modelling tradition, which emphasises the reality that all flows have effects on both sides of transactions.)

Within *sfc_models*, there are two types of open economy models.

1. One possibility is that all `Country` or `Region` objects share the same currency, and there are interactions between the countries/regions. (Formally, they are all included in the same `CurrencyZone` object.) From a coding perspective, this type of open economy model is not greatly different from closed economy models. Such models could be applied to truly federal countries (Canada, Australia, states within the United States), or even multi-country currency zones (particularly the euro area).

2. The second type is where the `Model` includes more than one currency (`CurrencyZone` object), and there are interactions between the currency zones. In this case, we need to add an `ExternalSector` object to the `Model`.

Note that we can embed multiple countries with different currencies into a model without requiring an `ExternalSector` object if there are no international transactions. What we have in this case are multiple closed economy models embedded within the same `Model` object. Although doing this may appear unusual, it allows us to run two similar models in parallel, and we are able to compare the results in the unified output.

There is one other interesting situation: where a single nation features transactions in multiple currencies. (For example, a developing country that conducts commerce in its local currency and the U.S. dollar.) Within the *sfc_models* framework, we can only model this by breaking the nation into different `Region` or `Country` objects with different currencies. Real-world sectors that conduct their business in multiple currencies would have to aggregate the behaviour of the different objects. The alternative implementation would be to enable multi-currency support within `Sector` objects, which would make code too complex.

6.2 Regional Models

Regional models are an interesting intermediate step between single-country models and multi-currency models. In these models, there are multiple `Country` objects, but they all share the same currency. It is possible to replace `Country` objects with `Region` objects in these models as a clarification, but Region objects are essentially equivalent to `Country` objects. (The only difference is that they use a default currency, which is the last currency created in the model.)

Regional models allow users to examine the economics of countries showing large regional differences (Canada being an obvious example), or even fixed exchange regimes like the euro. These models are much simpler than the multi-currency models, in that there is no need to translate currency values in exchanges that occur across currency zones.

The model REG (regional) from Chapter 6 of *Monetary Economics* is an example of such a model. This model was implemented in two ways within *sfc_models*, models REG and REG2. The two regions are labelled "North" and "South."

- `sfc_models.gl_book.chapter6.REG` implements the model within a single `Country` object. This method is much more complex, as there are many more sectors within the model, and we need to specify the connections between sectors by decorating the variables with "North" and "South."
- `sfc_models.gl_book.chapter6.REG2` implements the model using regions. The framework naturally tracks the naming convention for North and South for the user.

The rest of this chapter discusses multi-currency models.

6.3 Modelling a Gold Standard

Before discussing the code structure of multi-currency models, we will examine the economics behind the framework that is implemented in Version 1.0 of *sfc_models* – the Gold Standard.

Over the centuries, countries have followed many different patterns in how they organise trade and finance with other countries. In recent decades, the developed countries have had free-floating currencies and free capital flows. (The notable exception is the euro area, where multiple countries share a single currency. The euro floats freely versus other currencies, and there are few capital controls. However, the euro area has suffered crises relating the fixed currency relationship between the member countries.)

However, free-floating currencies are harder to model than a fixed currency regime within the *sfc_models* framework, as we need a mechanism to determine the price level of currencies. Doing so would require an extension to the equation solver, and this development was pushed to a version beyond 1.0. As such, this book only explains the implementation of the Gold Standard.

One of the difficulties of discussing the Gold Standard is that there were a number of regimes that are loosely referred to as a "Gold Standard." Furthermore, the idea is politically loaded, and a great many people view the Gold Standard as being "gold is money." However, this is not how the historic regimes, such as the Bretton Woods system, acted in practice. The modelling framework attempts to model the trade-offs faced by policymakers in systems like Bretton Woods.

The description here follows the description of model OPEN from Chapter 6 of Godley and Lavoie's *Monetary Economics*. We can interpret the results produced by sfc_models using the description here as well. However, the modelling strategy pursued by *sfc_models* is more complicated, as it is designed to be extensible towards a free-floating currency regime.

Using the standard `Sector` definitions from Version 1.0, the following assumptions are made about the Gold Standard system. (Comments in parentheses explain how these assumptions can be relaxed.)

1. There are strict capital controls; private sector entities cannot

hold financial assets from another currency zone. (This could be relaxed by having a sector set up a subsidiary object that holds financial assets for the parent. This would be relatively straightforward to do by adding equations to existing objects.)

2. Central banks are the only operators in the international gold market. (This would not be that difficult to relax; users can connect other sectors to the gold market by calling the `SetGold-Purchases` method.)

3. Central banks buy or sell gold in order to balance net flows in currencies.

4. Currency values are fixed (presumably by the central banks).

The latter two assumptions are not easily relaxed; doing so would require a new equation solution technique.

We can interpret the latter two assumptions as central banks requiring all other entities in the economy to use them as an intermediary for foreign exchange transactions.

This is illustrated in the following example. Imagine that Canada (currency code CAD) and the United States (currency code USD) follow the Gold Standard. We will now see the flow of goods and money that result from Canada importing goods from the United States.

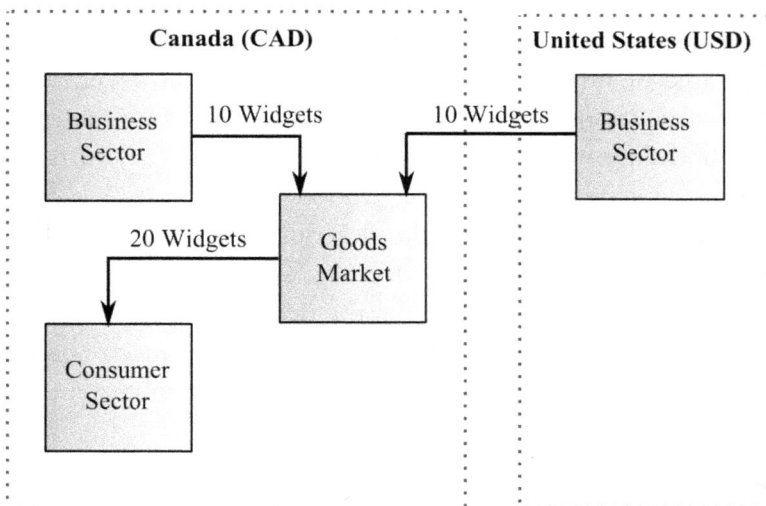

The previous figure shows the flow of real goods. The Canadian consumer sector consumes 20 widgets, 10 of which are produced by the domestic business sector; the remaining 10 are imported from the United States. Such a flow of real goods would happen regardless of the currency regime.

The "goods market" acts as an intermediary between the two business sectors and the household sector that is consuming produced goods. In the real world, this role would be filled by various retail firms. Within an economic model, this is just an abstract matching mechanism between the two supplying sectors and the consuming sector.

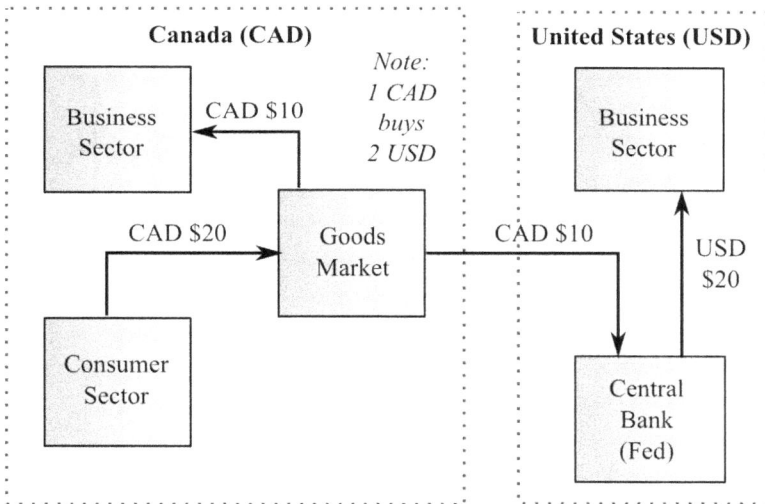

(Within the *sfc_models* framework, this of course is a `Market` object.) The differences of this hypothetical Gold Standard regime from the current free-floating regime appear in the figure above. The governments involved impose capital controls, and private sector entities are not allowed to hold foreign currency financial assets. Instead of the "Goods Market" paying the Business Sector directly (as it does the Canadian business sector), it sends the CAD $10 to the Central Bank in the United States (the Federal Reserve).

The governments in question are holding the exchange rate at 2 USD = 1 CAD, so that the 10 CAD is equivalent to USD $20, which the central bank sends on to the American business sector.

This outcome is extremely convenient for the *sfc_models* frame-work, as it preserves the fact that all cash flows received by sectors within the economy remain in the local currency of the country (the case of the central bank appears to be an exception; this is discussed next). This means that our accounting remains straightforward, as we do not have a mix of currencies within sectors' accounts.

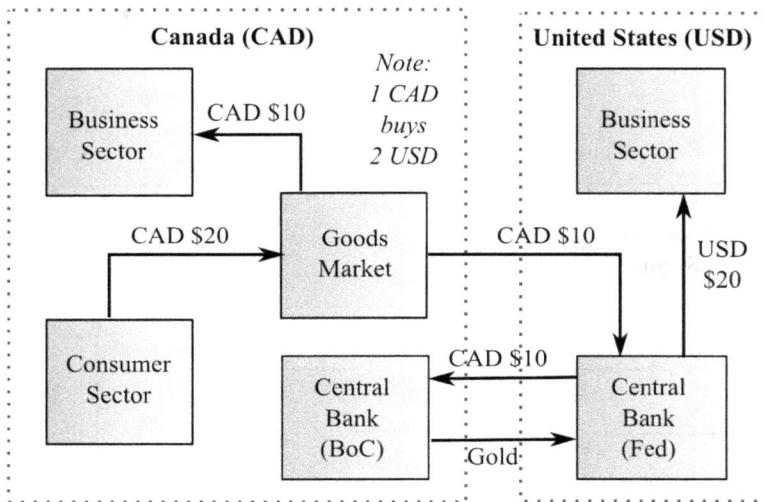

The exception that remains is the situation of the U.S. central bank. It is now holding CAD $10. In the real world, many developing central banks are in this position; they usually just hold the foreign currency as *currency reserves*. This possibility is not supported by the built-in class objects of Version 1.0, but such functionality would easily be added. We assume that memories of the War of 1812 remain fresh in this hypothetical world, and neither the Canadian nor the American government trusts each other enough to lend the other money (which holding financial reserve assets would entail). Instead, the governments demand that imbalances in foreign exchange be settled with gold. This is depicted in the figure above, which shows the final transactions that close the loop created by the importation of widgets. The Canadian dollars are shipped back to the Canadian central bank (the Bank of Canada) in exchange for CAD $10 worth of gold. Once this transaction is completed, we return to a situation where all economic sectors (including central banks) only hold domestic currency financial assets on their balance sheets at the end of the accounting period.

(In the Bretton Woods currency system that was adopted after World War II, gold was used as a last resort settlement mechanism. Most settlements were to be more easily traded U.S. dollars. From the perspective of foreign governments, both U.S. dollars and gold are assets that cannot be freely created. However, the United States is the monopoly supplier of U.S. dollars, which it could produce at no cost. This asymmetry was a core issue that helped lead to the demise of the Bretton Woods system.)

We can now see why thinking that a Gold Standard implies that "gold is money" is incorrect. The only entities that trade gold are central banks, and only to settle net flows. No one in the private sector ever touches a gold coin or bar, or even a direct claim on gold, at any point in the trade flow cycle. As will be discussed later the linkage between gold and financial assets – including "money" – can be quite tenuous.

In order to keep the diagrams tractable, only the case of imports from the United States to Canada was shown. However, so long as the United States did not have extremely stiff trade barriers, there would also be a flow of goods from the Canadian business sector to the United States. What matters for the balance in the currency market (and the net gold flows) is the net trade balance. So long as bilateral trade flows are balanced, imports and exports could be at any level without triggering gold flows.

If we assumed that the financial asset flows within the diagram are money – liabilities of the central bank – there is an interesting effect buried within the diagram.

- In Canada, Canadian dollars are returning to the central bank. Since an entity cannot hold its own liabilities as an asset (unless it can get a particularly shady accounting firm), what happens is that those returning flows cancel out existing liabilities. In other words, the Canadian money stock shrinks by CAD $10.
- In the United States, US $20 notes are being emitted by the central bank. This is a $20 addition to the USD money stock.

Within the discussion of Godley and Lavoie's *Monetary Economics*, the authors are able to show that the net trade in gold can be inferred by the changes to the central bank balance sheet. However, the *sfc_models* contains more equations specifying the net positioning of the foreign exchange markets, and the magnitude of gold sales is explicitly linked to them. The reason for the different treatment is explained in the next section, after the details of the *sfc_models* implementation are given.

It should also be noted that the framework is not limited to bilateral trade. It is straightforward to add more countries to a model; the `Gold-StandardGovernment` or `GoldStandardCentralBank` objects will also ensure that multi-lateral international flows are also balanced.

Since gold is a real asset, it seems clear that we cannot have negative holding quantities. There is nothing within the system of equations to prevent such an outcome (although the framework may eventually output warning diagnostics that the model is incoherent). This is not just a modelling problem; most attempts to peg currencies ultimately fail because the assets backing the currency regime fail, or the efforts to preserve the peg prove intolerable. Using fiscal austerity to protect gold reserves is discussed in Section 6.6.

6.4 Implementing Foreign Exchange in sfc_models

The implementation of foreign currency transactions within *sfc_models* is embedded in the `ExternalSector` class. This class is a subclass of `Country`, and it creates special objects that are subclasses of `Sector` to handle the various aspects of international transactions. The user is not expected to add objects to this abstract "country," although that might change because of extensions to the code base.

(The name `ExternalSector` is somewhat unfortunate as it is technically not a `Sector` subclass; however, the name seemed to be the most natural from the standpoint of economics jargon.)

In order to allow a model to support international transactions, the user needs to create an `ExternalSector` object, passing it a `Model` into which it is embedded.

```
obj = ExternalSector(model_object)
```

(It is not even necessary to assign to the variable `obj` if it is not accessed; the ExternalSector object will be embedded into `model_ob-`

`ject` within the constructor.)

Creating the `ExternalSector` will also create three `Sector` objects embedded within it.

1. An `ExchangeRates` object, with code XR. This class holds the various exchange rates within the model; the user can call `GetCrossRate()` to get the variable name for the exchange rate between two currencies. The embedded exchange rate variables can be adjusted to generate model scenarios.

2. A `ForexTransactions` object, with code FX. This object does the bulk of the work for the external sector, setting up the equations associated with cross-currency capital flows. The user will not normally deal with this object; instead, the framework will call it when cross-currency currency flows arise. (Either because of Market interactions or by registering cash flows.) If the user wants to extend the framework, an understanding of how this class operates would become a necessity.

3. An `InternationalGold` object, with code GOLD. This object handles gold transactions, which involve both flows stated in currency or volume (ounces) terms. The `GoldStandardCentralBank` and `GoldStandardGovernment` objects automatically set up their gold transactions, but the user may wish to add other sectors that interact with the gold market. This is done by calling the `SetGoldPurchases()` method, which registers a variable within a sector as representing the flow of gold purchases in local currency terms. (Gold sales are represented by negative purchases.)

The `ExternalSector` simplifies international transactions in multicurrency models by having it act as the intermediary for all cross-currency financial flows.

The left part of the next figure shows the original configuration of international financial flows in a three-country model. The diagram on the right shows how this is implemented within *sfc_models*: each original flow first enters the external sector, and then leaves the external sector to go to the original recipient. As a result, each country only has to look at its net flow versus the external sector, and not worry about aggregating across multiple bilateral relationships.

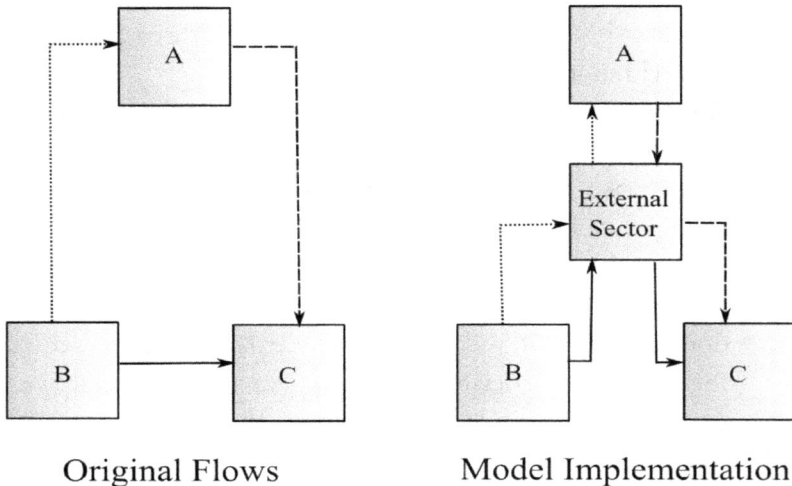

Original Flows   Model Implementation

(This is not a simplification if we indeed are only examining a two-currency model. It would be possible to create a bilateral foreign exchange object that emulates the behaviour of `ExternalSector`, but only allows for two currencies within the model. The resulting equations should be simpler. However, my preference was to implement the general multi-currency object before covering special cases.)

Having all transactions intermediated by this single abstract country greatly simplifies the thorny problem of keeping track of currency values, particularly in a multi-currency model. If we know that the exchange rate between the Australian dollar (AUD) and the Canadian dollar (CAD) is 1:1, and 1 CAD purchases 2 U.S. dollars (USD), we know that 1 AUD also purchases 2 USD. (We say that there is an *arbitrage* relationship between currency pairs.) Real world currency quotes incorporate a bid-offer spread, and so there is a small error bar around the ideal arbitrage-determined currency rates, but nobody can buy and sell at a price far removed from the theoretical fair value for very long without going out of business.

Even if we are not convinced by arbitrage arguments, we need to keep our currency values consistent if we want consistent accounting. For example, if we were not careful, we might set the bilateral exchanges rates between CAD and USD as:

- 1 CAD buys 1 USD; and

- 2 USD buy 1 CAD.

The values of financial flows are determined by multiplying the foreign currency value by the cross-currency rate (USD to CAD, or CAD to USD, depending on the direction of the flow). If we use incoherent prices like the above, the accounting will not add up. Effectively, some sector will have exchanged currency at the "wrong" value, and has suffered a capital gain or loss as a result. This gain or loss would effectively be pocketed by an unknown intermediary. The model accounting would therefore break down if the intermediary does not explicitly appear within the model.

Rather than force the user to make sure that exchange rate changes are coherent, the framework uses a simplification: all currency values are expressed versus a single unit of account. In the financial and economic literature, this single unit of account is known as a numéraire. As a result, the currency of the ExternalSector object is 'NUMERAIRE,' which has a currency value of 1 for all time by definition. Other currencies are then specified by a single time series, which is the number of units of NU-MERAIRE that can be purchased for 1 unit of the currency. The time series of these currencies is a variable within the exchange rate object ('XR'), with a variable name equal to the currency code.

This convention means that a larger currency value in the time series corresponds to a stronger currency. For example, if CAD goes from 1 to 2, it is stronger, since a single Canadian dollar can now purchase 2 'NU-MERAIRE' instead of 1.

Cross-rates have a variable name based on the two currencies, and they are calculated as the corresponding ratio of the two currencies versus NU-MERAIRE. Since there is no trade with the ExternalSector object, all sector economic behaviour should be based upon the cross-rates with "real" currencies.

This currency-naming scheme could trip up foreign currency experts. Currency rates can either be specified by naming the pair in full ("USD-GBP" for the U.S. dollar-to-British pound exchange rate), or by just specifying a non-dollar currency for the rate versus the U.S. dollar (which would be "GBP" for the previous example). That is, the U.S. dollar is treated as the numéraire, and not a fictitious currency. Unfortunately, the convention used (whether the rate specifies 1 USD versus x foreign, or x USD versus 1 foreign) appears random to the casual observer. (The conventions were determined by historical developments.) It would be ridiculous to emulate this haphazard approach, and so the *sfc_models* framework uses a consistent quote convention versus the NUMERAIRE.

Therefore, all that is needed to adjust currency values is to set the value of the currency versus the numeraire; cross-rate values will automatically adjust.

For example, we can do the following:

```
model_object.SetExogenous('EXT_XR', 'CAD',
'[1.]*5 + [1.2]*100')
```

This sets the variable CAD in the XR sector of EXT to be 1.0 for the first five periods (*k=0,...,4*) and 1.2 thereafter. This will cause CAD to appreciate versus all other currencies in the model (assuming the other currencies are themselves unchanged.)

As for international cash flows, these are normally handled within the framework; the user only needs to create an `ExternalSector` object. (If the object was not created, cross-currency cash flows will trigger a `LogicError` exception. We do not want to create the object if the user did not actually intend to have a cross-currency flow.)

There are two normal sources of cross-currency flows.

1. International sectors (exporters) may supply markets; the `Market` object will handle the cross-currency implications automatically. (There is currently no support for demand sectors to cross currency zones.)

2. The `RegisterCashFlow()` method of the `Model` object may be called, with the source and target sectors in different currency zones. The `Model` code detects that this is a cross-currency flow, and handles it accordingly. (Once again, it will throw a `LogicError` if the `ExternalSector` object was not created by the time cash flows are being processed.)

The following code uses `RegisterCashFlow` to create a cross-currency flow, it is probably the simplest possible way of generating such a flow.

File intro_6_04_externalsector.py:

```
from __future__ import print_function
from sfc_models.objects import *
```

```
from sfc_models.sector import Sector

mod = Model()
ExternalSector(mod)
ca = Country(mod, 'CA', currency='CAD')
us = Country(mod, 'US', currency='USD')

hh_ca = Sector(ca, 'HH', has_F=True)
hh_ca.AddVariable('GIFT', 'Sending money..', '5.')
hh_us = Sector(us, 'HH', has_F=True)
mod.RegisterCashFlow(hh_ca, hh_us, 'GIFT')
mod.main()
mod.TimeSeriesCutoff=1
series_list = ('CA_HH__F', 'US_HH__F',
'EXT_FX__NET_CAD', 'EXT_FX__NET_USD')
for s in series_list:
    print(s, mod.GetTimeSeries(s)[1])
```

What this code does is create two sectors, one in Canada, and the other in the United States. The variable GIFT is created, and set to be a constant 5.0. Then, a cash flow is registered, using the variable name GIFT as the value of the flow. (The value is in the source currency.)

The output is as follows:

```
CA_HH__F -5.0
US_HH__F 5.0
EXT_FX__NET_CAD 5.0
EXT_FX__NET_USD -5.0
```

When run, we see that the financial assets (F) in the Canadian sector are falling by 5.0 per period, while it is rising by 5.0 in the United States. (The exchange rates are set to 1 by default.)

However, something is wrong. The Canadian sector sends out 5 CAD, while the sector in the United States receives 5 USD. How was this possible?

Examination of the NET_CAD and NET_USD variables indicates the problem: they are non-zero. These variables indicate the net flows in each currency. If they are anything other than zero, there is an imbalance in foreign exchange transactions by the objects in the model.

One interpretation is that a non-modelled entity has acted as a financial intermediary for the modelled sectors, and so it ends up with net currency positions.

We can create GoldStandardGovernment objects in both countries to fix this imbalance. These sectors automatically balance the foreign exchange market, implicitly following the Gold Standard rules described in Section 6.3.

The new code is:

```
mod = Model()
ExternalSector(mod)
ca = Country(mod, 'CA', currency='CAD')
us = Country(mod, 'US', currency='USD')
gov_ca = GoldStandardGovernment(ca, 'GOV')
gov_us = GoldStandardGovernment(us, 'GOV')
# The need for the next step may be fixed...
gov_ca.AddVariable('T', 'Taxes', '0.')
gov_us.AddVariable('T', 'Taxes', '0.')


hh_ca = Sector(ca, 'HH', has_F=True)
hh_ca.AddVariable('GIFT', 'Sending money..', '5.')
hh_us = Sector(us, 'HH', has_F=True)
mod.RegisterCashFlow(hh_ca, hh_us, 'GIFT')
mod.main()
mod.TimeSeriesCutoff=1
series_list = ('CA_HH__F', 'US_HH__F',
'EXT_FX__NET_CAD', 'EXT_FX__NET_USD')
print('Net balance fixed')
for s in series_list:
    print(s, mod.GetTimeSeries(s)[1])

series_list = ('CA_GOV__GOLDPURCHASES',
'US_GOV__GOLDPURCHASES', )
print('Net balance fixed')
for s in series_list:
    print(s, mod.GetTimeSeries(s)[1])
```

The output is:

```
Net balance fixed
```

```
CA_HH__F -5.0
US_HH__F 5.0
EXT_FX__NET_CAD 8.93918681035e-05
EXT_FX__NET_USD -4.46959340517e-05
Net balance fixed
CA_GOV__GOLDPURCHASES -4.99995530407
US_GOV__GOLDPURCHASES 4.99991060813
```

We see that the net positions in CAD and USD are effectively zero (there is a small residual error in the model solution). This is achieved by the Canadian central bank selling 5 units of gold (PURCHASES are -5, that is, sales of gold) to the United States (PURCHASES are +5).

With this background material in place, it is now easier to explain the difference in the treatment of gold sales between Godley and Lavoie's *Monetary Economics* and *sfc_models*.

If we have a non-intermediated flow between two sectors that lie in different currency zones, there are two imbalances in aggregate balance sheets created.

1. The net flow of financial assets across the currency zone is no longer zero, as one currency zone is losing financial assets, and the other gaining.
2. The net flows in currencies are unbalanced.

The strategy in *Monetary Economics* is to argue that net flows in currencies are always zero by definition, and so they do not model them. Instead, the central bank buys or sells gold in order to keep the stock of financial assets balanced. (Since the central bank is the supplier of money, this is explained in terms of stocks of money and bills.) The fact that gold sales and purchases are balanced is an implicit result of accounting identities.

The strategy in *sfc_models* is for the gold standard governments to use gold sales to balance currency flows, and ignoring the domestic financial assets, as the foreign exchange transactions will implicitly cause the net flows of financial assets to net to zero.

The strategy of explicitly modelling the foreign exchange flows reflects the nature of the *sfc_models* package. As discussed in Chapter 7, *sfc_models* is meant to be used by researchers who will extend its capabilities. This requires flexibility, including the ability to modify any equation directly. As a result, it is to be expected that balance sheets identities will be violated, particularly during the development cycle. If the researcher causes financial assets to disappear from a domestic sector, that will show up in an imbalance in net financial assets. Effectively, there is a fictitious error flow implicitly created within the model. However, if the central bank automatically intervenes to balance domestic flows, there will be an imbalance created in the foreign exchange markets (since there was no international counterpart to the fictitious error flow). The researcher could then lose considerable time debugging the external components of the model they are building, not realising that it was a bug in the domestic sector construction that caused the problem.

6.5 Convergence issues

The action of the central bank in the gold standard operation is to cancel out imbalances in the demand for a currency. This creates some difficulties for solution convergence, which required an adjustment to the algorithm.

The net flows in a currency are given by:

Net Flows = (Non-central bank flows) + (central bank gold purchases).

We also want to enforce the relationship:

Net flows = 0.

Ideally, we would define gold sales as being the opposite of non-central bank flows (multiply by -1). However, this is a complicated expression, which varies from model to model. (If the equations were generated manually, this would not be a problem.)

It would have been possible to add a step during equation generation that determines the gold sales as a special case. However, a simpler equation form was chosen. The formula for central bank sales is given by:

Purchases = (Purchases) − (Net flows).

If we can find a solution, this obviously forces net flows to equal zero. However, we see that the function determining purchases involves multiplying the purchases variable by 1, and this seems to imply that the fixed point theorem condition (Section 4.4) is not applicable. In fact, the solution method fails, with the solution oscillating.

This lack of convergence was dealt with by modifying the solution algorithm.

1. At the beginning of the iteration, we start at a state vector *x*.
2. We calculate an estimated next state vector *y*, using the usual

rule. ($y = f(x)$).

3. The value for the next iteration is $w=(x+y)/2$. That is, the variables are only moved by half as much as suggested by the standard iterative solver. (Technically, this adjustment is only applied after the tenth iteration; the vector y is used early in the algorithm to speed initial convergence.)

By reducing how far the state vector jumps in each iteration, the algorithm was able to find a solution for the gold standard models tested.

This solution technique is heuristic, but since it widened the range of models for which convergence was achieved, it was left in place. It is expected that more advanced solution techniques from other Python modules will be investigated in the future.

6.6 The Gold Standard and Fiscal Austerity

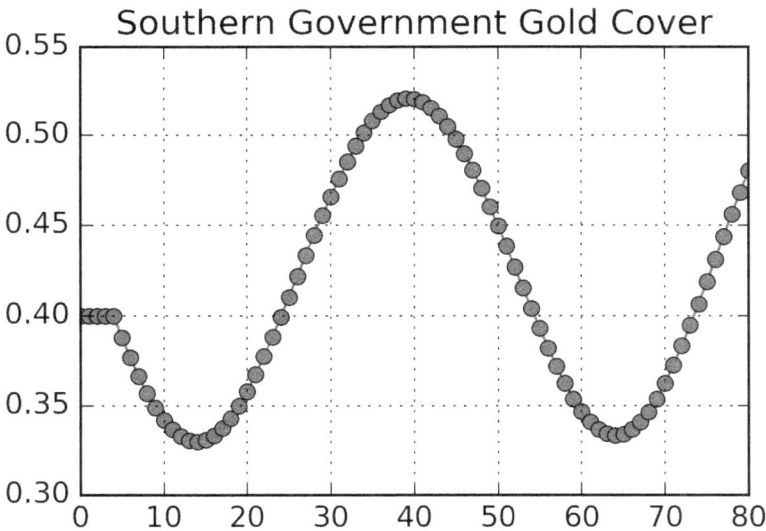

Southern Government Gold Cover

Although a Gold Standard is not exactly a pressing research topic, the simplicity of the system makes it easy to demonstrate ways in which we can use stock-flow consistent (SFC) models as *teaching models*. For example, we can explain why fiscal austerity policies are associated with the gold standard.

This model is based on model OPENG from Chapter 6 of *Monetary Economics* by Godley and Lavoie. I did not attempt to emulate the fiscal policy rules as laid out in the book, instead choosing to experiment with various possible settings. The example given here was one somewhat arbitrary example; I do not believe that the model outcomes are realistic. (I discuss how to extend the model in more realistic directions later.)

As in the book, the model is for two countries, labelled North and South. The model starts out in a steady state with balanced trade flows, but after a few time periods, the South experiences a jump in the *propensity to import*. (Translated from economist jargon, that means that a greater percentage of household income is spent on imports. Since imported goods are often luxury items, a rising propensity to import might reflect changing tastes as a result of rising prosperity.)

The chart at the beginning of this section shows the *gold cover* ratio for the South. In a gold standard, the monetary based is notionally backed by gold. The *gold cover* is the percentage of the value of money holdings that government gold holdings represent. (Keep in mind that under a gold standard, the value of the currency is pegged by the central bank to gold at a fixed value. Therefore, the gold cover cannot change as a result of the change of value of gold, so long as the pegged value does not change.) The gold cover starts out at 40%, which is the target level for the government.

(Some modern defenders of gold-backed money would object to describing this situation as being a "true" Gold Standard; under their preferred definition, the gold cover is forced to be 100% at all times. A gold cover of 40% would imply the dreaded concept of fractional reserve banking for gold, which is definitely not approved of. That is, all "money" is either gold coins, or a direct claim on a particular lump of gold. One could extend this model to cover such a situation. However, if we look at the gold exchange standard of the inter-war years, a partial gold cover was the norm. In other words, this section discusses a model gold standard that is operationally similar to historical gold standards, not the hoped-for system of gold money backers.)

Once the trade shock hits at time period 5, the gold cover starts to fall. This is because the South runs a trade deficit, and the central bank of the South has to sell gold to balance the foreign exchange market. The ratio later rebounds, and oscillates around the 40% mark. The question remains: how was this recovery in the gold cover engineered?

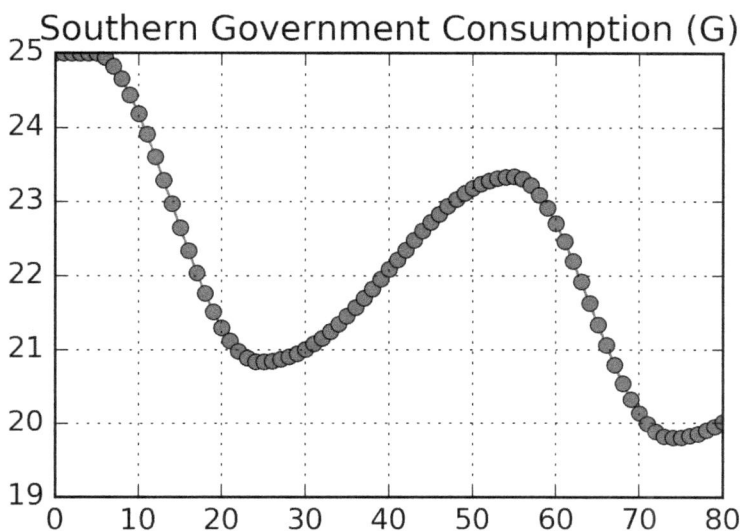

The chart above shows the policy lever that was moved to restore the gold cover. The Southern government cut back on spending (reducing G), following a mechanical rule that throttles back spending if the gold cover drops below target. Spending was steadily cut until about period 25, when it turned around. Spending oscillates over the longer term, but it is on a downward trend.

Looking at the time series data in detail (available in the text log files), we would realise that the cuts in government spending were too small to explain the improvement in the trade balance. Instead, the improvement in the trade balance was achieved by crushing the household sector. The chart below shows the after-tax income (disposable income) for the Southern household sector. Over the simulation interval, it fell from 100 to about 80, versus the much smaller decrease in government spending (25 to about 20).

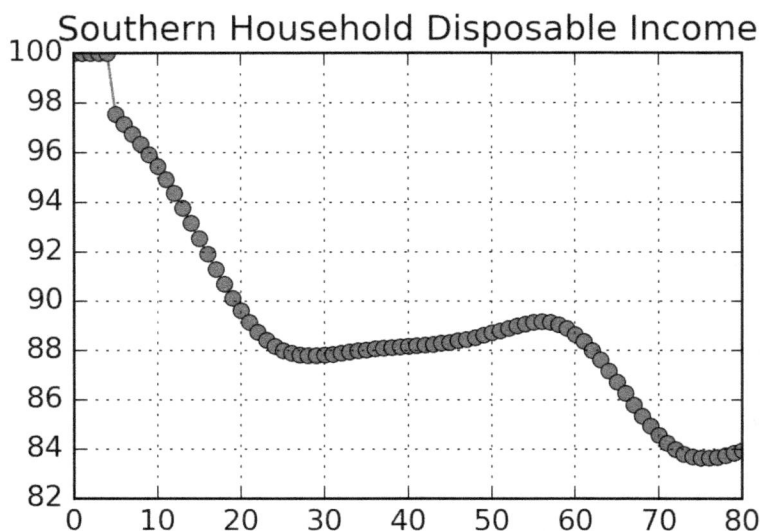

The situation in the North roughly mirrors the situation in the South. The next figure shows household disposable incomes in the North. Initially, the increased activity due to the export growth raises incomes in the North. However, once the austerity policy in the South improves the South's trade balance, the government of the North in turn has to implement austerity to improve its gold cover when it drops below target (also 40%). We thus get the oscillating gold flows seen in the first chart in this section. However, it should be noted that this is a negative sum game when looking at total incomes: both North and South households end up with disposable incomes below the starting level (100).

Northern Household Disposable Income

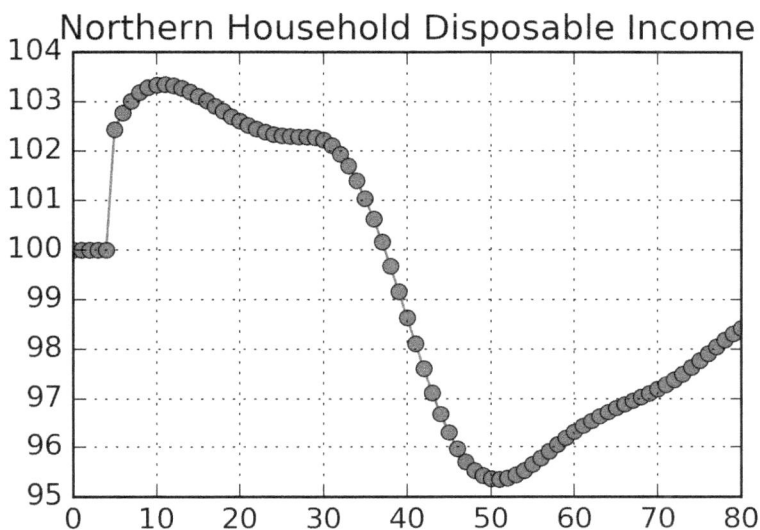

The outcome of declining incomes is the result of my choice to have the reaction of the government being asymmetric: spending is cut back more if the gold cover drops below target than if it rises above. This can be seen in the nonlinear specification of the variable ADJUST in the source code (below). Such an asymmetric reaction by authorities appears to be a reasonable approximation of the attitude of gold standard governments, but one could easily argue that I have stacked the deck against the gold standard.

The result is that we see a back-and-forth game of beggar-thy-neighbour policies. Nevertheless, we see that if policy makers care more about the gold cover than the welfare of their citizens, austerity policies achieved the stated objective of returning the gold cover ratio to target.

A model with slow-moving oscillations in financial variables is arguably unrealistic. Behaviour that is more realistic would likely involve the role of capital flows acting to speed up the adjustment process. In other words, there would be speculative attacks on currency pegs that are seen as unsustainable.

In order to implement such capital flows, the model would need to allow foreign sectors to own domestic financial assets. Such cross-border ownership is a standard feature of academic SFC models; it was not implemented in version 1.0 of *sfc_models*. In the gold standard behaviour currently implemented, the gold flows exactly offset real trade flows, hence net financial flows are zero. Once we allow cross-country financial asset holdings, both gold and financial flows would act as a counterpart to trade flows.

The mechanism for financial flows acting to replace gold flows is straightforward. If everyone believes that the currency exchange rate will remain pegged at the same level indefinitely, a higher-yielding foreign financial asset will be more attractive than a domestic financial asset. (Although we are thinking of both countries as pegging their currency value to gold, the result is that the exchange rate is also pegged.)

This creates a new policy lever to deal with trade imbalances. A central bank can hike its interest rate relative to the other central bank, which would induce purchases of domestic bonds. These purchases would help balance the foreign exchange market, reducing the amount of gold sales needed. As a result, there would be less direct pressure on the gold cover ratio. However, the higher interest rates would increase the fiscal deficit, and possibly reduce domestic economic activity. This means that interest rate policy only supplements the use of fiscal austerity to defend the gold cover ratio.

(In a floating currency world, higher nominal interest rates do not necessarily translate into higher bond returns. The higher carry can easily be offset by currency losses. Nevertheless, there seems to be an instinctive belief that central bank rate hikes should strengthen the currency, which is possibly a throwback to fixed exchange rate logic. As a disclaimer, I tend to assume that policy rate hikes coincide with a stronger currency, for a number of reasons which may or may not be true.)

Once we allow for these financial asset flows, it is not that difficult to extend towards models that resemble the operation of the euro area.

Even if one objects to the mechanics of this model, it provides a useful teaching example. By running the example code (given below, and in the examples folder), it is possible to examine the behaviour of all of the time series (and not just the few that I have highlighted here). Without seeing all the interactions, we are at the mercy of someone else's interpretation of economic events. In this case, we could imagine someone describing the policies undertaken here as "governments tightening their belts," which does not sound too objectionable to the untrained ear. When one realises that the actual "success" of the policy relies on a massive contraction in private sector incomes, one may look at this "belt tightening" in a new light. *(Alternatively, a fan of fiscal austerity might look at the simulation data and find objections to my interpretation.)*

File: intro_6_06_gold_standard_G.py

```
"""
intro_6_06_gold_standard_G.py

Model similar to model OPENG from Godley and
Lavoie's "Monetary Economics."

In this model, governments cut spending if they are
in danger of breaching their desired
gold cover ratio.
"""

from sfc_models.objects import *
from sfc_models.examples.Quick2DPlot import Quick-
2DPlot

def build_country(model, paramz):
    """
    Builds a country object.
    :param model: Model
    :param paramz: dict
    :return: None
    """
    country_name = paramz['Country Name']
    country = Country(model, code=paramz['Country'],
long_name=country_name)
    gov = GoldStandardGovernment(country, 'GOV',
initial_gold_stock=40.)
    #cb = CentralBank(country, 'CB', 'Central
Bank', tre)
    mm = MoneyMarket(country, issuer_short_
code='GOV')
    #dep = DepositMarket(country, issuer_short_
code='TRE')
    tax = TaxFlow(country, 'TF', 'TaxFlow',
taxrate=.2, taxes_paid_to='GOV')
```

```
    hh = Household(country, code='HH',
long_name='Household ' + country_name)
    goods = Market(country, 'GOOD', 'Goods market '
+ country_name)
    bus = FixedMarginBusinessMultiOutput(country,
'BUS', 'Business Sector', market_list=[goods, ],
profit_margin=0.0)
    goods.AddSupplier(bus)
    goods.AddVariable('MU', 'Propensity to import',
paramz['mu'])
    labour = Market(country, 'LAB',
'Labour market: ' + country_name)
    gov.AddInitialCondition('F', -100.)
    mm.AddInitialCondition('DEM_MON', 100.)
    hh.AddInitialCondition('F', 100.)
    gov.AddVariable('GOLDCOVER',
 'Gold Coverage of Money Stock', 'GOLD/SUP_MON')
    gov.AddVariable('LAG_COVER',
'Previous period''s GOLDCOVER', 'GOLDCOVER(k-1)')

    gov.AddInitialCondition('DEM_GOOD', 25.)

    gov.AddVariable('LAG_G',
'Previous period''s Government Consumption',
'DEM_GOOD(k-1)')
    gov.AddInitialCondition('LAG_G', 25.)
    if True:
        gov.AddVariable('ADJUST',
'Adjustmemt to spending',
'min(.2*(LAG_COVER-.4), .05*(LAG_COVER-.4))')
        gov.SetEquationRightHandSide('DEM_GOOD',
'LAG_G * (1 + ADJUST)')
    else:
        gov.SetEquationRightHandSide('DEM_GOOD',
'LAG_G')


def other_country(country):
```

```
    if country == 'N':
        return 'S'
    return 'N'


def generate_supply_allocation(mod, country):
    Y = mod[country]['HH'].GetVariableName('INC')
    other = other_country(country)
    market = mod[country]['GOOD']
    market.AddSupplier(mod[other]['BUS'],
'MU*{0}'.format(Y))
    mod[other]['BUS'].AddMarket(market)


def build_model():
    """

    :return: Model
    """
    model = Model()
    ExternalSector(model)

    paramz = {
        'Country': 'N',
        'Country Name': 'North',
        'alpha_income': .6,
        'alpha_fin': .4,
        'mu': '0.18761',
        'L0': '0.635',
        'L1': '5.',
        'L2': '.01',
    }
    build_country(model, paramz)
    paramz = {
        'Country': 'S',
        'Country Name': 'South',
        'alpha_income': .7,
        'alpha_fin': .3,
        'mu': '0.18761',
```

```
            'L0': '0.67',
            'L1': '6.',
            'L2': '.07',
        }
    build_country(model, paramz)
    generate_supply_allocation(model, 'N')
    generate_supply_allocation(model, 'S')
    # No longer using fixed G
    # model.AddExogenous('N_GOV', 'DEM_GOOD',
'[25.]*105')
    # model.AddExogenous('S_GOV', 'DEM_GOOD',
'[25.]*105')
    model.AddExogenous('S_GOOD', 'MU',
'[0.18761]*5 + [0.21] * 405')
    model.AddGlobalEquation('N_trade_balance',
'North trade balance',
'S_GOOD__SUP_N_BUS - N_GOOD__SUP_S_BUS')
    model.EquationSolver.MaxTime = 80
    model.EquationSolver.TraceStep = 5
    model.EquationSolver.ParameterSolveInitial-
SteadyState = True
    # model.EquationSolver.ParameterErrorTolerance
= 1e-4
    return model


def main():
    register_standard_logs('output', __file__)
    mod = build_model()
    mod.main()
    k = mod.GetTimeSeries('k')
    gc = mod.GetTimeSeries('S_GOV__GOLDCOVER')
    g = mod.GetTimeSeries('S_GOV__DEM_GOOD')
    Yd = mod.GetTimeSeries('S_HH__AfterTax')
    N_Yd = mod.GetTimeSeries('N_HH__AfterTax')
    Quick2DPlot(k,gc,
'Southern Government Gold Cover',
filename='intro_gold_cover.png')
    Quick2DPlot(k, g,
```

```
'Southern Government Consumption (G)',
filename='intro_gold_gov_spend.png\)
    Quick2DPlot(k, Yd,
'Southern Household Disposable Income',
filename='intro_gold_Yd.png')
    Quick2DPlot(k, N_Yd, 'Northern Household Dis-
posable Income',
filename='intro_gold_N_Yd.png')

if __name__ == '__main__':
    main()
```

Chapter 7 Extending the sfc_models Framework

7.1 Introduction

Although the objective of the *sfc_models* framework is to allow many interesting models to be built solely with the sector definitions that are pre-defined, researchers will need to extend the modelling capabilities in various directions in order to capture new features, or to replicate existing results in the academic literature.

At a technical level, there are two routes to achieving this aim.

1. The user can directly embed or overwrite equations within the model.
2. New functionality can be added by *subclassing* an existing class.

This chapter discusses how these strategies work, with an emphasis in subclassing, as this is a concept that may be unfamiliar for those without a programming background.

From a broader perspective, the *sfc_models* package is an open source package. Interested users can use the built-in collaboration tools to advance the package. Users can contribute examples, enhance documentation, report bugs or inconsistencies, or even contribute towards source code development.

7.2 Adding Equations

For the mathematically-inclined, the easiest way to extend the models generated by the package is to directly modify equations. To a certain extent, this is always necessary – for example, we typically need to set exogenous variables in order to generate interesting scenarios to analyse. However, it is possible to change behaviour more drastically by adding new equations to the dynamics.

This would usually be done after building a model that best corresponds to the plan for the finished model. The `Model` object generates a "final" set of equations that is the starting point for the modified model. Once the user knows the names of all of the existing variables, and how they relate to one another, it is now possible to start adding new relationships.

The first thing to keep in mind is that it is possible to change any equation, and you are free to try setting the equation to practically anything. The only hard limitation is that you need to keep the final block of equations in a format that the `EquationSolver` can solve. (This implicitly requires that you set the equations to be equivalent to blocks of valid Python code.)

This freedom comes at a cost – it is up to the user to ensure that the final set of equations makes sense. For example, if you arbitrarily increase the financial assets in one sector without making transactions in other sectors to compensate, you will end up with an incoherent set of balance sheets. At most, the framework will be able to diagnose the inconsistency once the system of equations is solved, and generate a warning message. (Such warnings are not implemented at the time of writing.)

This may sound surprising to some, as one of the characteristics of stock-flow consistent modelling is the emphasis on internally consistent accounting. However, the system is only generating a system of equations; it is not a simulation of underlying transactions – which would give it the ability to enforce the coherence of transactions.

The methods to set equations in a sector:

- `AddVariable()`
- `SetEquationRightHandSide()`
- `AddTerm()`

Global:

- `AddGlobalVariable()`
- `AddCashFlow()`

If the researcher sticks with the recommended high-level interface, the systems of equations will remain coherent. However, if they are manually changing equations, it is very difficult for the framework to detect that they do not respect accounting conventions. Implementing restrictions on the user's ability to interact with the equations would be a strategy favoured by other computer languages. However, users have access to the source code. Furthermore, it uses Python, a language that favours transparency and flexibility. The net result is that if safeguards were put in place to restrict how users set equations, the first thing those users would do is deactivate those safeguards. The real solution is to create a convenient high-level interface that incentivizes users to use them to build up accounting relationships coherently.

7.3 Adding Functions

By default, the equations within *sfc_models* can use the base mathematical operators in Python, or those within the math module, which is packaged with all standard Python installations. (The framework automatically imports the math module to allow the use of those operations. One implication is that the names of functions in the math module cannot be used as variable names.) In addition, it is possible to embed user-defined functions within equations. This allows for more complex mathematical operations than could be supported by the base mathematical operations.

Functions are added by invoking the AddFunction method of an EquationSolver object. (A Model object contains an Equation-Solver object as a member, with the same name.) The following is a simple example of AddFunction usage. It shows how a simple time-varying function can be implemented.

```
# Next line needed for Python 2.7
from __future__ import print_function
from sfc_models.equation_solver import
EquationSolver

def time_varying_function(k, x):
    if k < 2:
        return -x
    return x*x

obj = EquationSolver()
obj.ParseString('x=f(k, k)')
# Note: cannot use time_varying_function()!
obj.AddFunction('f', time_varying_function)
obj.Parser.MaxTime=3
obj.SolveEquation()
print('k', obj.TimeSeries['k'])
print('x', obj.TimeSeries['x'])
```

The program output:

```
k [0.0, 1.0, 2.0, 3.0]
x [0.0, -1.0, 4.0, 9.0]
```

As expected, the variable x is equal to -k for $k=0,1$, and k^2 for $k=2,3$.

The function is embedded into the solver by passing the function object into `AddFunction()`, you just need to make sure that you do not include function arguments, as that would call the function, and the return value of the function is embedded into the solver.

As this example illustrates, the name of the function within the model code is the first parameter to the `AddFunction` call, and can be different from the function as it is defined in the function code.

7.4 Subclassing

The preferred way to extend functionality within an object-oriented framework is to *subclass* an existing class. This creates a hierarchical relationship between the two classes, with the subclass inheriting the properties and methods of the parent class. This is greatly preferred to the common tactic of cutting and pasting existing code and then modifying it to add functionality.

There are two key advantages to extending *sfc_models* by subclassing. The first is that it greatly future-proofs your code. Any changes to the underlying functionality of the base classes should be inherited by the subclasses (unless the manner in which the subclass is designed overrides the new code). The second is that it reduces the number of lines of code to maintain.

This description of subclassing is the minimal amount that would allow the user to start creating new `Sector` classes. The Python documentation has a very good description of subclassing in Python, and would need to be consulted if you want to do more extensive development.

If you wish to create a new sector object by subclassing, you would need to find first a base class that covers most of the functionality you wish to incorporate. You then add functionality to your new class, changing the behaviour.

The code below is the definition of the `HouseholdWithExpectations` class, which adds the notion of expectations to the consumption equation (described in Section 5.4). This class is a subclass of the `Household` class. (This in turn is a subclass of the `BaseHousehold` class, which is a subclass of the Sector class, which ultimately is a subclass of the `EconomicObject` class. As one can see, subclassing is used extensively.)

```
class HouseholdWithExpectations(Household):
    """

    <Comment describing class>
    """


    def __init__(self, country, code, long_name='',
alpha_income=.7, alpha_fin=.3,
consumption_good_name='GOOD',
labour_name='LAB'):
        Household.__init__(self, country, code,
long_name=long_name, alpha_income=alpha_income,
alpha_fin=alpha_fin,
consumption_good_name=consumption_good_name)
        self.SetEquationRightHandSide('DEM_GOOD',
'AlphaIncome * EXP_AfterTax + AlphaFin * LAG_F')
        self.AddVariable('LAG_AfterTax',
'Lagged Aftertax income', 'AfterTax(k-1)')
        self.AddVariable('EXP_AfterTax',
'Expected Aftertax income', 'LAG_AfterTax')

    def _GenerateEquations(self):
        """
        Call base class to reset the Alpha
        variables.
        :return:
        """
        BaseHousehold._GenerateEquations(self)
```

This code example shows the three code segments that almost all sector subclasses will use.

```
class HouseholdWithExpectations(Household):
    """

    <Comment describing class>
    """
```

The first segment (above) is the class definition line. The fact that it is a class is denoted by the `class` keyword, the name of the class is given (`HouseholdWithExpectations`), and then in brackets the base (parent) class – `Household`. (It is possible to inherit from multiple classes, but I avoid that due to potentially complex issues that arise.) The class declaration is then followed by a documentation string that is embedded within the multi-line triple quotes (""").

```
def __init__(self, {variable list omitted here}):
        Household.__init__(self, {variables omitted})
        self.SetEquationRightHandSide('DEM_GOOD',
'AlphaIncome * EXP_AfterTax + AlphaFin * LAG_F')
        self.AddVariable('LAG_AfterTax',
'Lagged Aftertax income', 'AfterTax(k-1)')
        self.AddVariable('EXP_AfterTax',
'Expected Aftertax income', 'LAG_AfterTax')
```

The next code block is the __init__ method, which is called by default when an object of that class is created. The __init__ method is also called the *constructor*, since it is called whenever an object is constructed. (Unlike other languages, Python normally does not define the inverse operation – the destructor.) It is similar to a normal function, except that the first parameter passed refers to the object itself (normally denoted as self in Python). (I have omitted most of the variables from the function declarations in order to help formatting.)

- The first thing the __init__ method does is call the base class __init__, so that the object is properly initialised. (If this is skipped, the object will miss initialisation steps, and no longer mimic the base class.)
- Then, the next three lines add or modify equations associated with the sector. The first line overrides the existing equation for the demand for goods (DEM_GOOD); the difference is that DEM_GOOD now depends upon expected after-tax income (EXP_AfterTax), and not the actual after-tax income (AfterTax). The next two equations then define the equations that implement the EXP_AfterTax variable. (It is equal to the lag of AfterTax income.)

This has the same effect as manually overriding the equations in the Household class, but it is now embedded in a new class that can be easily re-used.

```
    def _GenerateEquations(self):
        """
        Call base class to reset the Alpha vari-
ables.
        :return:
        """
        BaseHousehold._GenerateEquations(self)
```

The last code block is the _GenerateEquations method. In this case, it calls the BaseHousehold GenerateEquations method, as this is needed to reset the "alpha" variables. (The need to make this call is not particularly obvious. This is done in case a user modifies the AlphaFin or AlphaIncome data members in the class. (For example, if hh is a HouseholdWithExpectations, the user might set hh.AlphaIncome = .65 in the code after construction. The BaseHousehold.GenerateEquations method will update the equations to match this change.)

All of the remaining methods that HouseholdWithExpectations inherited do not otherwise need to be modified. If subclassing were not used, all of the code from parent classes would have needed to be pasted into the object definition.

This example shows the typical workflow for creating subclasses. By using the existing sector definitions as examples, it should be relatively easy to create new sector definitions (once the equation generation system is understood). The only challenge is to determine whether equation definitions should be set in the __init__ method or _GenerateEquations. The rule is that if equations are defined using variables that are solely associated with the class itself, it can be safely defined in the constructor (__init__). Otherwise, since we do not know if the other sectors have been created yet, the equation definition should be held off until the GenerateEquations step (which is only called during the binding of the model, and all sectors have been created).

Appendix

A.1 Continuous Time Versus Discrete Time

One sometimes encounters *continuous time* economics, such as the Minsky package developed under the direction of the economist Steve Keen (URL: http://www.debtdeflation.com/blogs/minsky/). In a continuous time model, the time axis is the real line, instead of being discrete steps (as in the *sfc_models* package). This section discusses some of the advantages of the discrete time formalism.

The first key advantage of discrete time is that all economic and financial data are ultimately only available in discrete time. (This might be surprising for the case of finance, but it should be noted that the entire premise of the profitable high frequency trading industry rests upon the observation that financial transactions are not instantaneous. Continuous time models are used in mathematical finance, but these should be interpreted as approximations of the true system.) A continuous time model is therefore one step removed from the data, and we would have to be cautious translating properties that appear only in continuous time series.

Even comparing a discrete time model to data is always going to be a difficult process in practice. For example, how do we treat monthly data in a model that evolves quarterly? We are always going to lose information (or forced to insert information) as we change data frequencies. Furthermore, it is difficult to align data that are released with a variable lag to the calendar dates that they represent.

A second key advantage of discrete time is the simplicity of treatment, particularly if random variables are involved. As soon as we introduce randomness, it is incorrect to assume that the derivatives of any variables exist. To whatever extent solutions exist, they are defined in terms of Lebesgue integrals, a mathematical area that is not particularly well known. Almost all the work in analysis proofs would involve extremely obscure corner cases. ("What happens if government spending is \$20 if t is rational, \$0 otherwise?") It is one thing to define continuous time models where the components are passive resistances and capacitances that obey simple laws of physics; the interactions created by entities reacting in real time to inputs creates the possibility of highly pathological outcomes.

A related issue is the question of time delays. Within a discrete time model, a time delay is straightforward: we add a new state variable that is the original variable from the previous period. In continuous time, the amount of information contained within any non-zero interval is theoretically infinite. (For example, we could theoretically encode all human knowledge into a signal that lasts less than one microsecond. In practice, information channels have finite bandwidth, so we cannot achieve this.) In order to model a time delay, we have an infinite dimensional system. The statement of mathematical results (such as stability theorems) that apply to infinite dimensional nonlinear systems would comprise a very small book.

Finally, accounting is unusual within a continuous time system. We are no longer doing familiar accounting with stocks and flows that can be related with basic arithmetic. We instead would have to define all accounting relationships as stocks being the Lebesgue integral of flows. Such an environment is much less intuitive, and more prone to error. Furthermore, there is no clean way to model events that cause discrete jumps in stock variables, without invoking the Dirac Delta Function. This so-called function is not actually defined as a time variable, and so it is difficult to relate it to system behaviour that is defined as mathematical operations on time series.

The only real cost to discrete time analysis is that some of the more easily understood stability results (such as Lyapunov functions) are lost. However, it is possible to define the discrete time equivalents, and the general lack of computational tractability of such results for high dimensional systems makes the loss of this theory not practically significant.

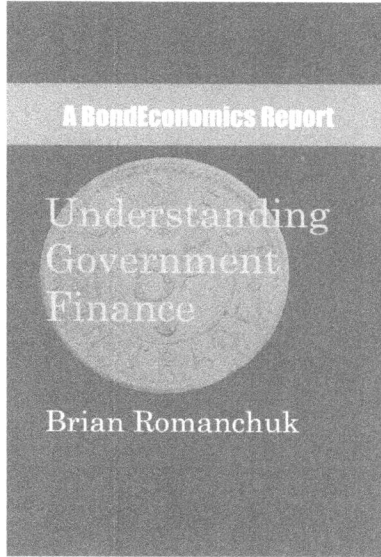

Understanding Government Finance (June 2015)
The government budget is not like a household budget. This report introduces the financial operations used by a central government with a free-floating currency, and explains how they differ from that of a household or corporation. The focus is on the types of constraints such a government faces.

This report introduces a simplified framework for the monetary system, along with the operating procedures that are associated with it. Some of the complications seen in real-world government finance are then added onto this simplified framework.

This report also acts as an introduction to some of the concepts used by Modern Monetary Theory, a school of thought within economics. Modern Monetary Theory emphasises the real limits of government action, as opposed to purely theoretical views about fiscal policy.

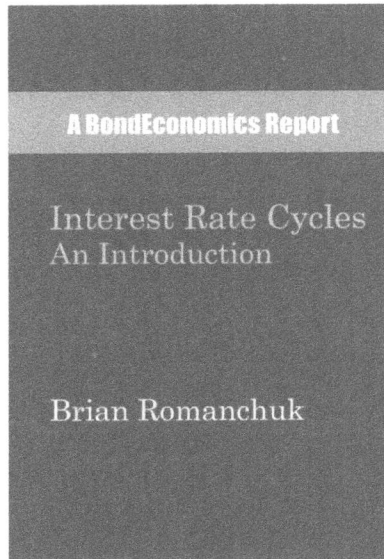

Interest Rate Cycles: An Introduction (June 2016)

Monetary policy has increasingly become the focus of economists and investors. This report describes the factors driving interest rates across the economic cycle. Written by an experienced fixed income analyst, it explains in straightforward terms the theory that lies behind central bank thinking. Although monetary theory appears complex and highly mathematical, the text explains how decisions still end up being based upon qualitative views about the state of the economy. The text makes heavy use of charts of historical data to illustrate economic concepts and modern monetary history. The report is informal, but contains references and suggestions for further reading.

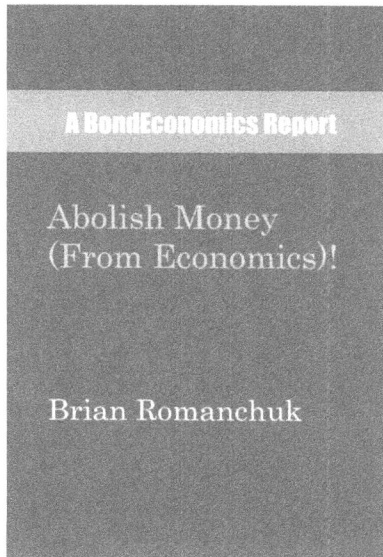

Abolish Money (From Economics)! (January 2017)

We live in a monetary economy, so it is not surprising that money plays an important role within economic theory. The argument of this book is that this role has become too important, and has warped our ability to think about the economy. The important psychological role of money within society has been transferred to monetary aggregates, and they are given far more significance than they deserve. Economists have wasted considerable time discussing reforms to the monetary system, such as Quantitative Easing, Positive Money, and Helicopter Money. We need to instead focus our attention on non-monetary reforms. This book consists of 22 essays that discuss the role of money within economic theory, and the controversies raised by debates about the role of money. The tone is informal, as the theoretical debates are translated into plain language.

About the Author

Brian Romanchuk founded *BondEconomics.com* in 2013. It is a website dedicated to providing analytical tools for the understanding of the bond markets and monetary economics.

He previously was a senior fixed income analyst at *la Caisse de dépôt et placement du Québec*. He held a few positions, including being the head of quantitative analysis for fixed income. He worked there from 2006-2013. Previously, he worked as a quantitative analyst at BCA Research, a Montréal-based economic-financial research consultancy, from 1998-2005. During that period, he developed a number of proprietary models for fixed income analysis, as well as covering the economies of a few developed countries.

Brian received a Ph.D. in Control Systems Engineering from the University of Cambridge, and held post-doctoral positions there and at McGill University. His undergraduate degree was in electrical engineering, from McGill. He is a CFA charter holder.

Brian currently lives in the greater Montréal area.

Index

Symbols

__file__ 30
_GenerateEquations 40, 125
__init__. See constructor

A

Abolish Money (From Economics)! 82
accounting identities 58
AddFunction 58, 121

B

BaseHousehold 40, 71
Bretton Woods 93, 97

C

Capitalists 42
CentralBank 46
Central Banks 81–85
closed economy 65
code complexity 14
code coverage 13
ConsolidatedGovernment 44
constructor 40, 41, 124
consumption function 71
continuous time 127
Contraction Mapping Theorem 59, 61
Country 32–34, 65, 91
CurrencyZone 32–33, 91

D

decorative variables 60
DepositMarket 48
deposits 84

E

EconomicObject 32–33
endogenous 55
endogenous money supply 84
end-to-end tests 66